D0678738

Knowing Words

A Guide to First-Year Writing and Rhetoric

Program for Writing and Rhetoric
University of Colorado at Boulder

HAYDEN
HM
McNEIL

Printed in the United States of America

10 9 8 7 6 5 4 3 2 1

ISBN 978-0-7380-2977-1

Hayden-McNeil Publishing
14903 Pilot Drive
Plymouth, MI 48170
www.hmpublishing.com

Pearce 2977-1 F08

PWR Contact Information

The PWR main office is located on the lower level of Environmental Design in Room 1B60. Our office hours are 8–12 and 1–5, Monday through Friday. We are closed on regular university holidays.

Main office (drop/add, general questions), 303-492-8188
Program Director, Patricia Sullivan, 303-735-5055
Associate Director of Upper-Division Writing, John Ackerman, 303-492-8015
Associate Director of the Writing Center, Steve Lamos, 303-735-5693
Associate Director of First-Year Writing, Patty Malesh, 303-735-4385
First-Year Coordinator, Lonni Pearce, 303-735-5654
Conflict Resolution Coordinator, Rebecca Dickson, 303-735-4908

Contents

Appendices

Introduction

About the PWR and First-Year Writing and Rhetoric

The Program for Writing and Rhetoric (PWR) is the center for writing instruction at the University of Colorado at Boulder. In addition to being a vital resource for writers on campus, the PWR is committed to excellence and diversity in learning and teaching; to creativity, scholarship, and community involvement; and to creating an atmosphere of openness and encouragement in the university and beyond. Our Writing Center provides writing support for students across campus.

T he program for Writing and Rhetoric offers three lower-division courses—WRTG 1100, WRTG 1150, and WRTG 1250—and a variety of upper-division courses. Descriptions of all our courses follow.

WRTG 1150 (3 credits). First-Year Writing and Rhetoric. Rhetorically informed introduction to college writing. Focuses on critical analysis, argument, inquiry, and information literacy. Taught as a writing workshop, the course places a premium on invention, drafting, and thoughtful revision. For placement criteria, see your advisor. Meets MAPS requirement for English. Approved for Arts and Sciences core curriculum: written communication.

WRTG 1100 (4 credits). Extended First-Year Writing and Rhetoric. Extended version of WRTG 1150, designed for students who want more preparation and practice in college writing. Meets the same goals and requirements as WRTG 1150, but with one extra hour of coursework per week to allow for more small-group and one-on-one instruction. For placement criteria, see your advisor.

WRTG 1250 (3 credits). Advanced First-Year Writing and Rhetoric. Advanced version of WRTG 1150, intended for more experienced writers. Meets the same goals and requirements as WRTG 1150, but at a more challenging level, including more complex reading and writing assignments. For placement criteria, see your advisor. Meets MAPS requirement for English.

WRTG 1840 (1–3 credits). Independent Study in Writing. Course created in collaboration with a PWR instructor and approved by the college. May not be used to fulfill core requirements.

WRTG 2020 (3 credits). Introduction to Creative Nonfiction. Explores from both the reader's and the writer's perspective the forms of creative nonfiction, including personal essay and memoir. Students will read and write extensively within this genre, develop skill in revision and peer critique, and learn how to submit work for publication. Prereq.: WRTG 1150 or equivalent (completion of lower-division writing requirement).

WRTG 2090 (3 credits). Electives in Writing. Explores a variety of academic and professional writing genres, ranging from research to technical writing, in intensive topic-focused workshops. Students will read and write extensively within their given genres, with an emphasis on developing a personal writing practice and exposing themselves to a broad range of writing modes. Designed for self-motivated students in a variety of majors.

WRTG 3007 (3 credits). Writing in the Visual Arts. Enables art and art history majors to improve their writing skills through organization, presentation, critique, and revision. Writing assignments include formal writing (analysis and argument), informal writing, and grant proposals. Formerly FINE 3007. Approved for Arts and Sciences core curriculum: written communication.

WRTG 3020 (3 credits). Topics in Writing. Through sustained inquiry into a selected topic or issue, students will practice advanced forms of academic writing. The course emphasizes analysis, criticism, and argument. Taught as a writing workshop, the course places a premium on substantive, thoughtful revision. Restricted to arts and sciences juniors and seniors. Same as NRLN 3020. Approved for Arts and Sciences core curriculum: written communication.

WRTG 3030 (3 credits). Writing on Science and Society. Through selected reading and writing assignments, students examine ethical and social issues that arise within the decision-making processes associated with science and technology. Focuses on critical thinking, analytical writing, and oral presentation. Taught as a writing workshop, the course emphasizes effective communication with both professional and non-technical audiences. Restricted to junior and senior engineering students and junior and senior physical and biological science majors. Approved for Arts and Sciences core curriculum: written communication.

WRTG 3035 (3 credits). Technical Communication and Design. Rhetorically informed introduction to technical writing that hones communication skills in the context of technical design activities. Treats design as a collaborative, user-oriented, problem-based activity, and technical communication as a rhetorically informed and persuasive design art. Taught as a writing workshop emphasizing critical thinking, revision, and oral presentation skills. Focuses on client-driven design projects and effective communication with multiple stakeholders. May be repeated up to 6 total credit hours. Restricted to juniors and seniors in engineering; architecture and planning; and the physical, earth, and life sciences. Approved for Arts and Sciences core curriculum: written communication.

WRTG 3040 (3 credits). Writing on Business and Society. Through selected reading and writing assignments, students examine ethical and social issues that arise within the decision-making processes associated with business and industry. Focuses on critical thinking, analytical writing, and oral presentation. Taught as a writing workshop, the course emphasizes effective communication with both professional and non-technical audiences. Restricted to junior and senior business students and junior and senior economics and IAFS majors. Approved for Arts and Sciences core curriculum: written communication.

WRTG 3090 (1–3 credits). Open Topics in Writing: Advanced. Advanced topics course providing intensive, specialized writing instruction in selected topics. Check with the PWR for current offerings. May be repeated for up to 6 total credit hours if topics are different. Prereq.: WRTG 3020, 3030, or 3040, or instructor consent.

WRTG 3840 (1–3 credits). Independent Study. Course created in collaboration with a PWR instructor and approved by the college. May be repeated for up to 8 total credit hours. May not be used to fulfill core requirements.

Why Take First-Year Writing and Rhetoric? (We Thought You'd Never Ask!)

To Know through Words

However you intend to use your education, you entered the university to gain knowledge. And knowledge is inseparable from words.

On the deepest level, we use words to understand who we are. Whether we're exploring the meaning of existence, the progression of history, the applications of math and science, or the behavior of the billions who download music from the Internet, we're using words to record experience, gather evidence, reason, feel, make decisions, gain skills, and grow. The more we understand about who we are, the better we understand not only how to make a living, but how to live.

> "Writing itself is an act of faith, and nothing else."
> —E.B. White

To Explore Who You Are as a Writer

Writing will be part of your learning experience over the entire course of your college career. What sets this course apart is that it invites you not only to work on improving your writing, but to explore and develop who you are *as a writer*.

Right now you may be thinking, "I'm not a writer. I write only when I have to." But consider: If someone asked you, "What kind of writer are you?" how would you respond? You might say that you like to write or you don't, that you're a particularly fast or slow writer,

> "I write to find out what
> I'm thinking about."
> —Edward Albee

that you dash off a writing task at the last minute, or that you start early (or stay up all night) and agonize over every word. Or, more likely, you may say that it depends—on the context, on whether you're interested in the topic, on who your readers are, on what your purpose is or how your writing is being judged. However you answer this question, the point is that you have an answer: a characteristic way of approaching writing, a set of habits, some you share with other writers and some that may be uniquely your own. And that makes you a writer.

To Find Your Own Reasons for Writing

There's something else that makes you a writer: Writers are people who have a reason to write. You may say that you

> "I write because I
> don't know what I
> think until I read
> what I say."
> —Flannery O'Connor

write only when you have to—but most writers would say the same thing. That "have to" can take several different forms—an idea, an inspiration, an assignment—and it can come from a number of different sources—a teacher, a boss, or yourself. Writers write for any number of reasons: to express themselves, to think "out loud," to persuade and inform others, to enter conversations beyond their own small circle. They write because writing is a way of making things happen, of changing hearts and minds—including their own. As a writer, you write because it is one of the best ways not only to tell others what you think and feel, but to *discover* what you think and feel.

The aim of this class, then, is to help you explore and expand your reasons for writing, to give you an opportunity to get to know yourself as a writer, to discover which writing habits have worked well for you in the past and to try new ones.

To Enter New Contexts and Cultures

If someone asked us to picture a typical "writer," most of us would conjure up an image of a solitary figure, lost in a world of his or her own, hunched over a piece of paper, staring into space, or looking for enlightenment in the glare of a computer screen. What this lonely image forgets, however, is that writing never takes place in a vacuum. We write not only for a reason, but for an audience, and the choices we make as we write determine whether we reach that audience.

This is basically what *rhetoric* means: writing with an understanding of the choices you have available to you as a writer and how those choices are always shaped by the contexts in which you write—who will read what you write and why. Whether you have a lot of writing experience or a little, college most likely represents a new writing context for you, one that brings with it a new set of challenges. The purpose of this course is to help you meet those challenges.

> *"It's hard for me to believe that the first semester of my college career is already coming to a close. I started not knowing what to do and have ended with a sense of understanding about my new surroundings. This sentiment applies not only to my college experiences so far but [also to] my work in [this] class. With each paper, I started out perplexed, and by the end, somehow I gained clarity and understanding of my topic. Each project forced me to push my writing abilities to different limits."*
> —Tracy Stientjes, WRTG 1150 student

Entering college means you are bringing yourself into a classroom where new questions will challenge you to find deeper, more complex answers. The flurry of questions can obscure the fact that the answers begin with you—with the self that steps into a lecture hall or a workshop or a library, the self that takes notes, reads, discusses, and sits down at a computer. You bring to every question a reservoir of experiences, beliefs, motivations, and dreams, moved in mysterious ways by your genes, your desires, your culture, what you eat (and drink), and how much you sleep.

To Engage Knowledge

Lecture halls can give you the impression that you're here to absorb knowledge. The First-Year Writing workshop introduces you to the process of *engaging* knowledge—bringing an awareness of your own perspective into dialogues with minds you've never encountered before. Your perspective may be strengthened, reshaped, or even transformed, but it will still be yours. The soundness of your perspective—throughout the entire undergraduate process of developing it—will depend on your ability to draw upon the work of other people and gauge its validity and value, as you form your sense of self as well as your contribution to the many communities that surround you. This is what it is to think academically.

A central purpose of academic thinking is to inform the civic discussions that shape our communities. First-Year Writing and Rhetoric challenges you to think academically, engage in academic discussions with your teachers and peers, recognize the audiences who can benefit from your education, and convey your insights in forms of communication that are persuasive and productive. Your writing workshop is a short course in what it is to know yourself and to take your place as an informed, thoughtful member of your communities.

Learning Objectives: How They Break Down

First-Year Writing and Rhetoric is organized around five main learning objectives.

Objectives	How You'll Meet Them
To write with fluency; to acquire a practical and reflective understanding of the writing process.	• You'll write frequently, generating writing on a variety of subjects for different purposes and from different perspectives. • You'll compose a series of essays that will enable you to explore and gain practice in all aspects of the writing process, from choosing a viable topic to developing and shaping your material to refining your final draft for your readers. • You'll also have frequent opportunities to workshop writing in progress with your peers and to confer with your instructor in individual conferences. • You may also be asked to write short reflective pieces about your writing—about your process and progress, breakthroughs and setbacks. The reflective pieces will help make your learning more visible to you and will help you articulate the kinds of feedback that will be most helpful from your peers and instructor.
To acquire rhetorical sensitivity, making informed choices as you adapt your writing to the needs of your readers, to a specific context and situation, and for a particular purpose.	• In-class exercises, analyses of readings, and workshops on your own and other writers' drafts will help you learn to situate your writing within a larger communicative context—personal, academic, and civic. • As you analyze your own reasons for writing a specific piece, you will take into consideration the needs, expectations, and perspectives of readers who may not share your vantage point, your experience, or your knowledge about your subject.

To become a proficient reader, approaching texts with a writer's awareness of craft and a critic's ability to interpret and respond to a text's meaning and effects.	• You'll analyze the strategies with which writers explore their subjects and express meaning—a published author's voice, arguments, evidence, and style. • You'll respond to the text based on your own experience, knowledge, questions, and beliefs about what an author is saying and doing, thus interacting with the text as a reader who shares responsibility with the author for a text's meanings and implications. • You'll talk and write back, lending your own critiques and insights to the cultural conversations stimulated by the various authors you read.
To develop strategies of research that will enable you to become an active investigator of your culture.	• You'll investigate a subject that attracts and intrigues you. • You'll learn how to formulate and pose a question, problem, or issue for research; how to uncover what is already known about your subject; how to choose an appropriate method or strategy for your own research; how to analyze data and determine the credibility and validity of your sources; and how best to convey both the information you've uncovered and your own discoveries in an essay intended to inform and persuade other readers.
To understand and apply conventions of standard linguistic usage, including proper grammar, syntax, and punctuation, as you compose, revise, and edit your writing across a range of rhetorical tasks and genres.	• Through workshops, conferences, and your instructor's comments on your drafts, you will become informed of errors you're making and ways to correct them. • You'll be instructed in how to use your assigned writing handbook for self-directed learning as you're composing, formatting, or editing your writing on your own. • Your instructor will devote class time to the basic structures of syntax and punctuation in standard English, and to common errors and their correction. You'll be encouraged to take responsibility for your respect or disrespect for conventions of standard English usage.

If that sounds like a lot to learn in one semester...well, that's because it is. But you're not expected to learn it all at once. As you'll read in the next chapter, you'll work toward these objectives through what we call "the four Rs": reading, writing, research, and reflection. Like the three Rs you learned in grade school—reading, writing, and 'rithmetic—these aren't the kinds of things that you master overnight, but rather practices that you keep learning all your life.

Critical Inquiry

Conducting Inquiry, Creating Community

ll first-year writing courses share a common curriculum, which is to say that they are "about" the same thing: critical inquiry and community.

Conducting Inquiry

First-Year Writing and Rhetoric is structured around a sequence of writing assignments that build on one another. While the particular assignment sequence may vary from section to section, depending on your teacher, all sections are designed with two primary aims in mind. The first we have already talked about, and that is to give you experience writing for a number of different audiences and purposes—personal, academic, and civic. The second is to introduce you to the ways of reading, writing, and thinking known as *critical inquiry*.

What Is Critical Inquiry?

If you've turned on the TV or opened a paper lately, you know that many of the current discussions in our culture tend to fall into what might be called binary thinking: either/or, pro/con, left/right, true/false. Critical inquiry challenges us to go beyond the usual binaries by looking for the shades of gray—and red and turquoise and purple and chartreuse—that black-and-white thinking blocks out. It challenges us to suspend judgment for long enough to consider more fully what is at stake and for whom. It challenges us to seek other perspectives as we work to formulate our own. And it challenges us to strike a healthy balance between skepticism and curiosity, so that we may come to more informed, less predictable, perhaps even surprising conclusions.

> *"We do not write what we know; we write what we want to find out."*
> — Wallace Stevens

How Does Critical Inquiry Happen?

Three processes make up critical inquiry: analysis, argument, and inquiry. None of these processes can be separated fully from the others.

• **Analysis** breaks a thing up into its component parts and asks how they work together. Imagine a chemist who encounters an unknown substance. Right away, she'll ask, "What is it made of? How does its composition determine its specific properties—the ways it interacts with other substances?" That is, *why* does it behave the way it does? Anything that has parts can be analyzed: a physical process, a social institution, a work of art, a document. You learn to write partly by analyzing writing, including your own. What makes an argument persuasive (or not), what makes a political cartoon both funny and critical, what beliefs or assumptions are behind a particular policy statement?

> *"We do not write in order to be understood; we write in order to understand."*
> — C. Day Lewis

Notice that, although they start with the word *what*, these are all really *why* questions. A *why* inquiry makes a good start for analytical thinking. Analysis may take off from an existing discussion, but it can also ask an entirely new question—and that's when it's at its most intellectually exciting.

The biggest challenge in analytical writing is to come up with an original interpretation, not just an obvious description. Here's one rule of thumb: If your thesis comes to you in less than half an hour and feels safe, it isn't analytical. Analyzing a document can be especially tricky, because you must find a meaning that's not obvious on the face of the text—not just a summary. And originality entails risk. You have to be willing to say something that others might disagree with, and then persuade them to agree instead. In other words, you must argue. In fact, the best way to deepen an analysis is to argue with yourself.

It can be tempting to disguise your analysis as mere description, on the assumption that your readers will be more willing to agree with you if they think what you're offering them is "just the facts." This is the tactic usually adopted in propaganda. The propagandist does not want to call attention to his or her own role in interpreting the facts. The analytical thinker, in contrast, must distinguish honestly among facts, assumptions, and his or her own interpretations. That's because the propagandist's aim is merely to secure the reader's assent, by any means, fair or foul; the analytical thinker's aim is to secure the reader's rational assent.

• **Argument** often gets a bad rap in our culture. We may think of two sides, each trying to win by shouting the other down. But most arguments worth engaging in have more than two sides, and an effective argument doesn't shout. In critical inquiry, an argument isn't something you win or lose, but a process aimed at advancing the discussion. It is as much deliberative as persuasive.

Argument assumes a real opponent who is worthy of being taken seriously (and quoted fairly!). It also assumes a reader who is a party to the existing conversation and therefore already has a point of view—one that needs to be changed. You should take this as a challenge, not a threat. Just as some philosophers tell us that without the freedom to do wrong there's no real virtue, so without the possibility of disagreement there's no possibility of genuine assent.

It's easier to change minds if you share some common ground with the opposition and make some concessions. It helps to assume a calm and reasonable tone. And it's vital to address the arguments on the other side—the "counterarguments." Here's one way to think of this process:

"Although others argue (A, B), I
- grant (A)
- oppose (B) on the following grounds . . .
- present arguments (C, D, E, F) on my own side."

Beware of arguments that merely talk past the counterarguments, like this:

"Although others argue (A, B), I
- present arguments (C, D, E, F) on my own side."

Notice, too, that a good argument seldom just rearranges various claims that have already been made by others; instead, it makes a new, analytical contribution to the ongoing discussion.

As you construct your own arguments, you'll need first to analyze the values, assumptions, and evidence behind your claim, and also to account for perspectives other than your own. This is what makes argument so critical to both academic and civic culture.

• **Inquiry** means more than just searching the library for answers. Real inquiry is interactive; it requires you to construct your own answer. Furthermore, as you've probably noticed, writing tends to be much more engaging when it not only issues from genuine curiosity but sparks our own curiosity in return. Sometimes the best answer is a new question.

> "A writer who waits for ideal conditions under which to work will die without putting a word to paper."
> —E.B. White

Different academic disciplines engage in inquiry in different ways; in fact, academic disciplines are in part defined by the kinds of questions they ask and the ways they go about investigating them. But inquiry is important far beyond the walls of the university. Consider: What if no one had ever questioned the assumptions behind racial segregation, or asked why the world is getting warmer?

There are two opposite pitfalls in conducting an inquiry: hunting for evidence to bolster your own preconceived idea, and uncritically absorbing the views of whatever writer you happen to be reading at the moment. Research is more productive if you allow some time for serendipity, for unexpected changes in your own focus; but haphazard research and passive reading seldom get you anywhere.

To see some ways that other student writers have used analysis, argument, and inquiry, see the student writing samples in Chapter 5.

Creating Community

F irst-Year Writing and Rhetoric is likely to be smaller, livelier, and louder than your other courses. It is also likely to demand more active involvement from you. Why? Because writers grow and improve by working with other writers.

To encourage writers to work with one another, the course is taught as a cross between a reading seminar and a writing workshop. Writing workshops will give you a chance to read your writing through others' eyes and to learn new strategies by seeing how other writers work, while class discussions will provide a forum to test your thinking, to practice listening to what others have to say, and to talk through your writing. The community you create will not be confined to the classroom. The collaborative work you begin in class will spill over into your instructor's office hours, discussions over e-mail, and—we hope—talk in coffee shops and dorm rooms.

The writer's worst enemy is self-absorption, an unwillingness to look beyond ourselves or to look at our work in new ways. A writing workshop can help us expand our personal and intellectual horizons by encouraging us to switch roles, to inhabit the minds and imaginations of others. This role-switching stretches us. As in all communities, the members of your class may not always agree with one another. The goal is not agreement but understanding and, of course, clearer expression. You will work together to challenge and support one another, to help one another grow as writers.

Knowing Through Words: "The Four Rs"

A s human beings, we have developed language as a means for knowing—for understanding ourselves and our world. Although this is a writing course, writing is only one "R" in a process of understanding that also requires reading, research, and reflection.

Reading

First-Year Writing and Rhetoric is grounded in reading—assigned readings, sources you find through your own research, and the texts written by other students in the class. Discussions and writing assignments will require you to read critically—to discern not just information but the author's reasoning, so that you can respond more thoughtfully with your own questions and insights. Are there holes or confusion in the argument? Does the text connect with your own experience? Your response might take the form of a class debate, an analysis of an article, a persuasive paper based on research, or an oral or written critique of the work of one of your peers. You'll also practice reading like a writer, tuning in to how other writers convey their meaning. Good musicians listen carefully, not only to the music, but also to *how* that music is made.

Writing

First-Year Writing and Rhetoric takes you through all parts of the writing process—finding a topic worth writing about, defining your audience, asking questions, understanding the roots of your own thinking, gathering and weighing the validity of information and

> *"I'm rewriting it while I'm writing it. It's changing itself."*
> —Max Apple

arguments, reconsidering your views, expressing and substantiating them, and experimenting with structure and language to find the most effective way to convey what you mean. In writing workshops, with the entire class or in smaller groups, you'll discuss drafts of one another's papers. You may also discuss your plans for research and writing, read your work out loud, or write evaluations of the work of your peers. In light of the feedback you receive, you'll revise.

Experienced writers know that the writing process is unpredictable and recursive; it "runs back" on itself. As your piece evolves, you will discover the need to loop back to an "earlier stage" of the process, inventing again, revising again, editing again, in whatever order is necessary. As you discuss drafts in workshops, you and your peers will explore ways to focus your meaning for a particular audience. Readers tell us whether our writing is doing what we want it to do. The best writers are rewriters.

For more information on workshops and revision, see Chapter 4.

Research

Many assignments for First-Year Writing and Rhetoric will require research. The course introduces you to campus resources, methods of research, and criteria for determining the credibility and validity of your sources. Inquiry-driven research involves substantially more than compiling information. It requires cultivating curiosity.

> *"In baseball you only get three swings and you're out. In rewriting, you get almost as many swings as you want and you know, sooner or later, you'll hit the ball."*
> —Neil Simon

Your experience may be a starting place for inquiry into the roots of your own values and perspectives. But curiosity will also take you into other times and places—other generations, cultures, religions, classes, levels of education, and areas of expertise. When you understand your own position and step back to examine it from other perspectives, you can reinforce or reshape your own views with more confidence and authority.

For more information on some of the resources you can use to do research, see Chapter 3 and the Library Resources section in Appendix B.

"I try to leave out the parts that people skip."
—Elmore Leonard

Reflection

Throughout the processes of reading, writing, and researching for this course, you will be asked to reflect on what you are doing. In class discussions, conferences with your instructor, journal entries, or short essays, you will cultivate the habit of thinking about the choices you make as a reader, a writer, and a researcher, so that you can become more conscious of those choices, more in control of how they work.

The questions you ask as you read make you aware of how you are entering a conversation or dialogue with the text. How am I responding intellectually and emotionally? Do I agree or disagree? Why? How does this connect to my own experience and observations? What is foreign and new? What confuses me? Why? What gives me new insight? How?

The questions you ask as you write help you understand your relationship to the subject you are exploring. On the deepest level, what do I think about this issue? Are my evidence and reasoning honest? Am I asking relevant questions? Am I using my own voice? What subjects and issues compel me enough to read, research, and write about them? How can I cultivate curiosity? What parts of this writing task am I resisting and why?

"I'm happy when the revisions are big. I'm not speaking of stylistic revisions, but of revisions in my own understanding."
—Saul Bellow

The questions you ask as you research are driven by the demands of the issue as well as your own curiosity. What is the current thinking on this issue? How rapidly does it change, and why? What are the competing points of view? Who has the expertise to speak with authority? What are the strengths and weaknesses in the arguments from each point of view? What topics have been left out of the debate?

As you gain mastery in the process of reading, writing, and researching, you'll learn to ask deeper, more relevant questions, and you'll become more adept at answering them. Reflection will become a habit of mind.

Chapter 3

Information Literacy

Getting Information, Getting Over Information Overload

In order to conduct an inquiry of any kind, you need to know how to find information—facts and fresh perspectives that will speak to whatever question is driving your inquiry. You'll also need to know what to do with that information once you have it. Toward that end, your class will work closely with University Libraries to help you cultivate what is known as "information literacy."

Information Literacy: What Is It?

I f you've ever typed a friend's name into a search engine and come up with 40,347 hits, or if you've ever typed a research topic into a library database and come up with a list of 1,028 books on the subject, then you know: It isn't hard to find a lot of information fast. We live in the Information Age, when information has a way of *finding us*.

Just using a search engine isn't the shortcut it first appears to be, since the information you find tends to overwhelm your original research question. This method often leads to information overload—how will you ever sort through all of these sources? And how will you evaluate the quality of the information?

The challenge is finding information you actually want and knowing what to do with it once you find it. That's basically what information literacy is about. Information literacy helps you

- establish your research need;
- select relevant sources;
- evaluate those sources.

We know better than to believe a headline in the *National Enquirer* about Oprah's evil twin or the latest all-lettuce diet. But it isn't always so easy to know what to make of information found in, say, *The New York Times, The Journal of the American Medical Association, Time* magazine, or a webpage on gun control. What information can you trust? How do you put that information into perspective? How credible is the author? What is his or her agenda?

There are five major steps to information literacy:

Step	Example 1	Example 2
1st Step: You realize you need information to answer a question, resolve a problem, or finish a project.	You are writing a paper on endangered species in Colorado and need information on the topic.	You have problems getting your landlord to fix the safety violations in your apartment on the Hill.
2nd Step: You efficiently find the needed information.	You search Chinook, the library catalog, and find half a dozen books and 10 government documents about endangered animals in Colorado. You then search the Internet to find a Colorado State Government webpage about indigenous animals and their population size.	You search out the relevant regulations and appropriate government institutions. You discover that the City of Boulder has a Rental Housing Licensing and Inspection Program.
3rd Step: You evaluate the information gathered.	You notice that one of the documents you found is from 1981 and its statistics are no longer current.	You notice that the Boulder Revised Code, including the Housing Code, Rental Licenses, and Occupancy Restrictions, is on that department's website. You compare the Code to the specifics of your situation.
4th Step: You use the information effectively to accomplish a specific purpose.	You write your eight-page paper on Colorado's endangered species population, including statistics, reasons for the endangerment, and ways to alleviate the problem.	You document the violations in your apartment and your attempts to get them fixed.
5th Step: You understand the legal and ethical issues surrounding the use of information.	You use quotations or some form of acknowledgment when using others' words or ideas, and you include a bibliography at the end of your paper.	You pursue your case with the relevant authorities, informing your landlord of your intention to do so.

Developing Information Literacy

Information literacy instruction for First-Year Writing and Rhetoric begins with a series of online tutorials and quizzes known as RIOT, for Research Instruction Online Tutorial.

Tutorials: There are four tutorials:

1. "Think"—how to establish a search strategy.

2. "Find"—how to find books, scholarly articles, and newspaper articles using the university's online databases.

3. "Evaluate"—how to evaluate the credibility, validity, and relevance of the sources you find.

4. "Cite"—how and when to cite sources in order to avoid plagiarism and add to your credibility as a writer.

Throughout the tutorials, you'll answer quiz questions. When you complete each tutorial, your answers to the quiz questions will be graded by the library and e-mailed to you and your instructor.

To find RIOT, go to

http://ucblibraries.colorado.edu/pwr/tutorial/home.htm.
For more information on RIOT and other library resources, see the Library Resources section in Appendix B.

Once you complete the tutorials, you'll be prepared for the library seminar. The seminar is designed to
- give you a chance to research a subject you're working on for class;
- build on what you learned in the tutorials, but show you more complex and more advanced research strategies;
- allow you to work in person with a library staff person who can guide you in the right direction for your own research.

Here's how the seminar works:
- Your instructor will schedule the seminar during your regular class time. Your class will meet in the library.
- A library staff person will review important ideas from the online tutorials, and then introduce you to more advanced research techniques.

The rest of the class time will be devoted to a kind of "live" research session, where you will be able to ask library staff for help with your research.

> In addition to resources that your instructor and the library staff provide, you can find a list of online writing and research resources on the PWR website at http://www.colorado.edu/pwr/resources.html. Click on "Writing and Research Links."

Chapter 4

Workshops and Revision

Workshops and revision are two important, closely related activities. For **workshops** to succeed, you'll need to be able to offer—and be willing to receive—constructive criticism. **Revision** is an ongoing process that involves a lot more than running a spell-check and fixing those pesky grammatical errors. This section explains common myths about workshopping and revision, and it offers advice about what you can do to make both of these crucial processes effective.

Workshop Guidelines

Workshops will play a key role in the course, so you'll want to know how to make the most of them. Whether your instructor asks you to discuss your writing in pairs, in small groups, or as a whole class—or uses a combination of these approaches—workshops will give you a good idea of what's working well in your writing, as well as what you need to rethink and revise.

Just as importantly, workshops will help you refine your skills as a critical reader. By learning to help your classmates improve their writing, you'll become a better reader of your own work, which will in turn make you a more confident and successful writer.

First let's consider two common myths about workshops. If you go into a workshop with a negative attitude based on one of these myths, you might miss a great opportunity to improve your writing and help your peers improve theirs.

Common Myths about Workshops

Myth #1: *I'm not qualified to comment on someone else's draft.* You might think, "I'm no expert when it comes to writing, so who am I to criticize someone else's draft?" The assumption here is that you have to be a superb writer yourself, or at least highly trained in the craft of writing, to have something valuable to say. This just isn't the case. In fact, as a general, educated reader, you can give invaluable feedback.

> *Tip*: **Trust your instincts as a reader**. Just because you're not a published writer or a writing instructor doesn't mean that your thoughts and suggestions don't matter. Everyone writes for an audience, and as a reader you're a legitimate member of one. When reading someone's draft, don't waste too much time correcting grammatical errors. Focus instead on more important issues, such as how persuasive you find the writer's argument, how effective the supporting evidence is, and how compelling the organization is.

Myth #2: *Our opinions don't matter anyway, because our instructor will be the one who grades our essays*. Although it's true that your instructor will grade your essays, that doesn't mean that you and your peers can't help one another improve your writing. Chances are, if you find a classmate's argument unclear, so will your instructor. Likewise, if a peer thinks that your draft is poorly organized, don't be surprised if your instructor agrees.

Tip: **Have confidence in your ability to help your classmates improve their writing, and respect their constructive criticism**. Of course, you might not end up using every suggestion you get. After all, one person might love your title and appreciate its sense of humor, while another might find it unprofessional and inappropriate. Rather than throw up your hands in frustration when you get conflicting advice, think about each disputed issue and decide for yourself whose advice to follow. Finally, keep in mind that your instructor probably won't be able to read and respond to every draft you write, so you'll often *need* to rely on the advice of your peers.

What Makes a Good Workshop?

Here's what some CU–Boulder first-year writing students had to say about the qualities that make a workshop successful:

Positive Attitude

- "A good workshop is when people bring their writing and are open and willing to have discussion about it. People have to be willing to accept, or at least acknowledge, criticism. That's the only way people are going to get better at writing, by accepting critical help."
  —Mike Ramsey, WRTG 1100

Preparation

- "In my opinion a good workshop means that everyone in the class comes prepared. If there are only a few people who are wanting to workshop, then it won't be fun and you will not get the proper feedback."
  —Kristen Hanson, WRTG 1100

Honesty

- "In the past I've always had workshops or small groups where they only tell you good things about your paper for fear of hurting each other's feelings. This year, however, I received good criticism on my papers because it was honest. In order for this method to work, you have to be open-minded and willing to accept someone else's thoughts or opinions."
  —Casey Stokely, WRTG 1150

Specific Criticism

- "Constructive criticism is the best way to collect other people's opinions on your paper, and vice versa. Be sure to give specific examples of what you liked, disliked, and what could be improved. It's more helpful to know what you did wrong when revising and editing."
  —Tiffany Valdez, WRTG 1150

Focus

- "I really dislike it when people constantly get off subject. It's great to hear discussion, but only if it involves a critical discussion of the person's paper; otherwise it seems pretty pointless."

  —Emily Lumia, WRTG 1150

Balance of Praise and Criticism

- "The workshops that were most helpful were the ones where I received comments about the strengths and weaknesses of my paper."

  —Johnny Laychaypha, WRTG 1150

By keeping this advice in mind, you can make a huge difference in the dynamics of your class throughout the semester. Will you be the person who reads a draft and says things like "It's good. You just need to fix a few commas"? Or will you be the person who genuinely tries to help your classmates by saying things like "The organization is clear overall, but you could use a stronger transition between the second and third paragraphs"? Will you talk about last weekend's big game, or will you talk about the need to address credible counterarguments? When it comes right down to it, your attitude and effort will make or break your workshops. So why not help make them positive learning experiences for yourself and your classmates?

Revision

So you've just spent two weeks—or four or six or 13—working on a piece of writing. You've done your research, you've workshopped drafts in class, you've conferenced with your instructor. And on top of that, all five of your roommates read your paper and told you it's great. You're done. Right?

Well, maybe not. Your instructor is telling you that you still need to revise your paper. Whether you're at the end of a long drafting process or at the beginning, you can expect to revise your writing many times along the way. To some writers, this sounds tedious and frustrating—but hold on! Instead of thinking of revision as a chore, think of it as a golden opportunity to make your writing better. You now have the chance to reread and reflect on what you've written, think about what you *really* want to say, and make whatever changes are necessary to improve your original work.

What Is Revision?

Revision literally means to re-envision, to see again. When you revise a piece of writing, you step back from your work and look at it again through new eyes. Now is the time to think about how readers will experience your writing, how other people will respond to your words and ideas.

Common Myths about Revision

Myth #1: *Revision means fixing the mistakes*. Many writers mistake "revising" for proofreading—in other words, running a spell-check on your computer or skimming your paper to look for typos or grammatical errors in the last few minutes before you turn your paper in for a grade. But revision is much more than that. Proofreading is one *part* of the revising process, but a successful revision can be anything from a change in the word choice or sentence structure to a radical change in content to a complete overhaul of the organization of your essay—among many other options.

> *Tip*: **Keep an open mind as you revise**. Believe it or not, you may even benefit from doing more freewriting to generate new ideas. Some people even write entirely new essays, inspired by one key idea they had in their original essay. Revision is the process of rethinking your essay, top to bottom, and choosing what elements of your writing you want to improve. Every time you look at a piece of writing, you'll probably come up with new ideas!

Myth #2: *Revision is always the last thing you do after you've completely finished a piece of writing*. Many writers think that revision comes only at the very end of the writing process, but really, you begin to revise almost as soon as you put the first few words on the page. You may write your first few sentences, decide they don't really say what you mean, and go back and rewrite those same sentences.

> *"While in the first draft you're writing for yourself, in the second draft you begin to let go of the piece for the sake of what it can offer to others."*
> —*Bonni Goldberg*

> *Tip*: **Remember that writing is a recursive and generative process, meaning you use writing to figure out what you're thinking about a topic**. As you write, you often sharpen your thinking and develop new ideas or new ways of seeing old ideas. Then you put those new ideas on paper, which in turn generate even newer ones. So really, revision *is* writing; writing *is* revision.

Myth #3: *Good writers don't need to revise because they get it right the first time*. Some students see revision as a sort of punishment, as if the teacher is telling them to revise because they're not good enough and they need to work harder than the "good" students. The truth is, *all* writers revise. No, let's amend (er, revise) that: all *good* writers revise. Writers know that their first ideas are just the beginning. No first draft ever sees the light of day. Writing is a long process that takes time and effort and lots of thinking and rethinking.

> *Tip*: **Take heart in the fact that each time you write, you become a better writer**. So each time you revisit a piece, you are revisiting it as a better writer than you were when you wrote the previous draft. The more you practice, the better you get—and the more skills and insight you can bring to successive drafts of your writing.

What Students Say about Revision

"Revising a piece of writing is the chance to do the 'coulda, shoulda, woulda' that you wish you had the time or thoughts for. I almost always find *something* I wish I had done differently, either just at the time I turn the paper in or in rereading it after the paper is graded and returned. Revising is your second chance to get it just the way you want it to be."
—Jean Rice, WRTG 1100

"Revision is a unique process for me. My final draft is completely transformed from my original draft. During the revision process, I come up with new ideas, and abandon old ones. After I have organized my thoughts, the last step in the process is to check for grammatical errors."
—Steve Bonner, WRTG 1150

"Revising takes raw ideas and turns them into coherent ideas."
—Bo Dodd, WRTG 1100

"Revising is when you clean up your thoughts on paper. The first draft is a conversation with yourself, the other drafts are for other people. I revise a lot because I always get new ideas and have a new outlook every time I reread a paper."
—Kaitlin Bernstein, WRTG 1100

In addition to resources that your instructor and the library staff provide, you can find a list of online writing and research resources on the PWR website at http://www.colorado.edu/pwr/resources.html. Click on "Writing and Research Links."

Are You a Writer or an Editor? Both!

At professional publications such as newspapers and magazines, multiple people contribute to every piece published. A story may have only one byline, but really, it has been produced by a team. Here's an example of how writers and editors may work collaboratively to produce a story:

•**Writer**: When the writer first comes up with an idea or gets an assignment, she pairs up with an editor to brainstorm ideas and figure out what sources to turn to for information.

•**Content Editor**: After the writer produces a draft, an editor will review it and send it back to the writer, asking her to make significant content changes, such as adding more information or rewriting entire sections. Often the writer and editor will work through several (or several dozen) drafts together.

•**Copy Editor**: When the writer and editor are confident that the content of the story is as good as it can be, the story goes to a copy editor, who reviews it for clarity, cohesion, flow, and wording. The copy editor will often consult with the writer to clarify ideas or sentences that may be confusing.

•**Proofreader**: Finally, the piece of writing goes to a proofreader, who reads it for correctness, making sure the grammar, spelling, and punctuation are perfect.

By the time the story is printed, it has usually been read and commented on by four people—and revised too many times to count!

In the same way, you play these different roles when you revise your writing. Although you'll work with other people—your instructor, other students in your class, friends—to revise your work, ultimately, you serve as your own content editor, copy editor, and proofreader.

Revision Checklist
Here are some questions to consider as you think about what elements of your essay you want to revise.

Audience Awareness

Rhetorical Situation
☑ Do I have a strong purpose for writing this essay?
☑ Is the relationship among audience, purpose, and content appropriate and effective?

Appealing to Readers
☑ Do I effectively engage my readers?
☑ Do I appeal to my readers' logic and emotions?
☑ Do I establish my ethos as a writer?

Voice and Style
☑ Is the voice in the writing appropriate for the subject, purpose, and audience of this piece?
☑ Is the style of my writing appropriate for the subject, purpose, and audience of this piece?

Content

Ideas
☑ What do I really want to say in this paper? Do I say it?
☑ Is anything missing?
☑ Do I make enough points? Give enough examples?
☑ Could I go back and do any more research? Are there any other stories from my personal experience that I might include?
☑ Could I add more description or concrete, sensory details?

Meaning
☑ Does this essay have a strong sense of significance?
☑ Is there enough evidence to support the thesis (or controlling idea) of this essay?
☑ Is my reasoning sound, accurate, and convincing?

Focus
☑ Is my thesis (or controlling idea) clear, strong, specific, and sophisticated?
☑ Does all the information work to develop and support the controlling idea?
☑ Overall, is the writing thorough and compelling?
☑ Is all the information here relevant? Is anything superfluous or irrelevant or redundant?

Organization and Clarity

Introduction and Conclusion
- ☑ Could the introduction do anything more to engage the reader, establish the tone, and set up the controlling idea of the paper?
- ☑ Does the conclusion bring a satisfying sense of closure?

Structure
- ☑ Do I as a writer deliberately lead the reader through the essay in a clear, logical way?
- ☑ Is the information presented in the best possible order?
- ☑ Is there any redundancy of words, phrases, sentences, or ideas?

Paragraphs and Transitions
- ☑ Does each paragraph focus on one main topic? Is that topic relevant to the thesis of the paper?
- ☑ Are the transitions between paragraphs clear and logical?
- ☑ Does each sentence connect to the one that came before it and the one that follows?

Style
- ☑ Is the prose lively, engaging, and sophisticated?
- ☑ Is the voice consistent throughout the essay?
- ☑ Are all the words I've chosen accurate and clear? Are my vocabulary and diction appropriate and effective?

Conventions of Language

Sentence structure
- ☑ Does each sentence make sense and sound good?
- ☑ Are sentences well-constructed, effective, and varied?
- ☑ Are there too many short, choppy sentences? Too many long, wordy sentences?

Mechanics and Grammar
- ☑ Are the punctuation and spelling correct?
- ☑ Are there any grammatical errors?

Citation of Sources
- ☑ If the essay refers to outside sources, are they cited correctly in the text?
- ☑ Is the Works Cited or bibliography properly formatted?

Student Writing Samples

The following collection of sample essays shows how important student writing is for all first-year PWR courses. As you read the samples, you'll see how these student writers situated themselves, first and foremost, as *writers*. In your class, you'll experience different types of and occasions for writing, and you'll often use your own and your peers' essays in an ongoing discussion about writing and writing topics. Each piece that follows is very different from the others, with the focus and approach varying according to the purpose of the essay. A common thread in each is something you will likely encounter in all good writing: clarity, conciseness, and a strong sense of the writer behind the ideas and words.

We selected the following essays according to six categories—personal narrative, analysis, inquiry, argument, persuasion and rhetorical analysis, and reflection—because you will often encounter these forms of writing in your courses. Understand that these categories are not strict boundaries but rather genres that often bump up against one another depending on the purpose and occasion for writing. The most imaginative student writing often weaves something of each category to meet the demands of the subject and audience. Each essay presents a good opportunity to engage the writer and the many occasions for writing.

*Relation between herself ⸮ a book.
*Very honest. Vulnerability
*Suprise - US being foreign.

Personal Narrative American *Girl lives in Hong Kong, comes*
Sample Essay 1   *back to American culture*
                                        feels out of place.
WRTG 1250
Instructor: Rolf Norgaard

With the informal theme for the class being "Culture and Identity," Jocelyn Liipfert developed a personal narrative that drew on her years of
experience living in Hong Kong. By analyzing her own experience
and extending it to a set of experiences shared by so-called "third-cul-
ture kids," Jocelyn explores the tensions that surround the process of
growing up in an increasingly multicultural world, thereby linking her
personal experience to a larger social issue.

Cultural Chameleon

JOCELYN LIIPFERT

For me, being late to school meant chasing down taxis at 7:15 a.m. and hurriedly telling the driver, in broken Cantonese, to please hurry. A day of shopping meant searching the Hong Kong market streets for a pair of shoes larger than a size 7 and bargaining for thirty minutes with the shopkeeper to bring the price down to less than ten dollars. Lunch with a friend was being the only white girl in a small noodle house tainted by the smell of the ducks and chickens hanging in the window, my voice drowned out by music blaring through Cantonese speakers. Sometime in the five years I had lived in Hong Kong, between speaking a little Cantonese and knowing the downtown streets like the back of my hand, I was promoted from my status as a typical American blonde to a true Hong Kong kid. When I moved away the summer after my sopho-more year in high school, I was leaving home and going somewhere completely foreign.

Texas.

I will always remember the first day of public school. My mom dropped me off at the front of the school, as kids sped by us in their huge SUVs to viciously snag a parking space. Inside, I was met with a swarm of Aber-crombie-clad blondes and brunettes in every hall and at every corner. My thoughts were drowned out by singing of the latest songs on the radio, gossip, and laughter. Seeing as these were people who spoke the same native language as me, who looked the same and sounded the same, you would think that I would finally feel at home and relieved. But I had never felt so *foreign* in my life.

This American culture which my parents called their own did not at all feel like something that was mine. I was confused by the fact that I felt more at home and at ease in a culture where I stuck out as blatantly different than in one where I blended in completely. It was this challenge and these feelings that established me as what is commonly referred to as one of the world's "Third Culture Kids." In their book so titled, David C. Pollock and Ruth E. Van Reken describe in detail the concept of what it means to grow up in a culture other than that of your own native culture, and the challenges and emotions that are often met. My mom had given me a copy of this book a couple days after that horrific first day, and I found myself intrigued by the challenges it described. It surprised me that there was actually a name for my experience, and that the descriptions in the book matched exactly what I was experiencing at that particular moment in time. Pollock and Van Reken define a Third Culture Kid (TCK) as

> a person who has spent a significant part of [his or her] developmental years outside the parents' culture. The TCK builds relationships to all of the cultures, while not having full ownership to any. Although elements from each culture are assimilated into the TCK's life experience, the sense of belonging is in relationship to others of similar background. (19)

Children of businessmen, "military brats," and study-abroad students all fit this profile and, upon return to their home country, are confronted by both the benefits and challenges wrought by their experience. They find themselves deeply affected by "this weaving together of [their] two dominant realities" (78).

I could strongly relate to the benefits and challenges described by Pollock and Van Reken, including an expanded worldview met by confused loyalties, a three-dimensional take on the world met by a painful view of reality, cross-cultural enrichment met by ignorance of the home culture, adaptability met by a desperate attempt to define differences between cultures, and knowledge of the "outside world" accompanied by sheer arrogance.

Although TCKs often benefit from the expanded worldview they gain from spending time in a foreign country, they also simultaneously gain a set of confused loyalties. I found that because of my experience attending an international school in Hong Kong, I encountered a huge blend of people from various backgrounds. My best friend was Dutch South African and would often talk about her family being evacuated due to rioting rebels. A Chilean classmate would take an extra month off school during winter to go home for her summer. I became accustomed to the religious practices of my Hindu, Muslim and Buddhist friends. While in context it seemed normal, I look back now and realize how living in such an international setting made me more open-minded and perceptive not only to other cultures, but to the various beliefs and philosophies people of my own culture possess. Harboring this open-mindedness also brought on a strange sense of confusion.

Being one of few Americans at my international school, my habits and subconscious rituals, accent and appearance labeled me as an American to my peers. Wearing this label also came with a responsibility. Every time my president was criticized, or some catastrophic event occurred in the US, I always felt obligated to explain or defend my country, regardless of whether I really believed or supported the circumstances. I felt like it was my responsibility to educate people as to why my country did something this way, or to justify our actions. When the US would involve itself in the conflict of another country, I would often find myself in heated debate as to why my country was doing what it was doing. While personally I didn't always advocate or support US actions, I felt I had to at least force these people who were criticizing the US to entertain another possibility, another reason that led to such actions. I felt as though their criticisms of Bill Clinton or George Bush were criticisms of *me*. However, when I moved to Texas, my position was quite different. I didn't feel *at all* American, and I felt instead a representative of the perspectives of the rest of the world. I was entirely offended when someone assumed that Hong Kong was part of Japan, or asked me if I rode in a rickshaw to school. It was so frustrating—I felt like I was an American in China, yet Chinese in America. Pollock and Reken describe this feeling as a "confusion of loyalty" that many TCKs experience, and "can make them unwelcome citizens in their own countries" (83). I think in my frustration with Texas, I failed to realize that here I was preaching about the rest of the world's perspectives and how Americans need to be more open-minded, yet was at the same time being completely *close*-minded towards my own country. It *was* hard trying to assimilate back into my own culture, and frustrating to deal with my classmates' ignorance of the world. Yet over time I realized how hypocritical and unsympathetic I was being, and how I had alienated myself and made it even more difficult to add onto and grow from my experience. Once I became more aware of how I was being perceived by others, I made an effort to be more understanding, receptive, and patient to the people of the culture I call my own.

Aside from confronting a quality of acceptance and a quality of frustration, TCKs also develop a different kind of perspective of the world. In addition to witnessing cultural differences, TCKs see the world in a way that "is impossible to do through reading books, seeing movies or watching nightly newscasts" (83). Because of the things TCKs experience—sights, smells, and feelings in regard to situations they are put in—watching the news or a movie can bring back these senses in the form of a "3-D panoramic picture show" (84). Daily news topics become more real and visually stimulating to TCKs than to their non-TCK peers. This same ability also brings on a more painful sense of reality. Pollock and Reken describe a painful reality that a TCK may experience in watching the news: because of their "heightened senses," a TCK realizes that behind the screen are real, living, breathing people. Watching the news can often seem redundant to people who have lived in their native country their entire lives. The pictures of suffering Middle Eastern women have recently been pervasive throughout the news and magazines. Their abundance has caused many viewers to become desensitized to their reality. To someone who has never been to the Middle East, these faces are often surreal and exist as though they are a removed reality. However, a TCK who had lived in the Middle East sees a real woman, in real pain, in a place that is familiar. The women they see on the flat screen resemble the women they saw in everyday life, in shops and markets. They resemble the faces of their maids, a friend, or a waitress from their favorite restaurant. To them, bombs are more real than scenes in a movie and are more meaningful than the statistics run off on the nightly news (85).

While TCKs gain knowledge and understanding of the various cultures outside theirs, they are often found to have a profound ignorance towards their native culture. I could give an in-depth breakdown on the history of politics and government in China; however, I could not begin to speak with any shred of knowledge in regard to US politics. I remember one particular experience when I had first moved to Texas and was having dinner with a few friends. One girl was also a TCK and had lived in Shanghai for a number of years, and the other two girls were Texas born and bred. My Shanghai friend and I were joking around about how one of the Texas girls thought the capital of China was Hong Kong. That was *crazy* to me that someone could not know the capital of the most heavily populated country in the world, not to mention that China reigns as a world power. But then the girls turned around and asked me if I knew the capital of Texas, and in all honesty, I couldn't say. At the time it seemed to me inconsequential information, as Texas represents only a small fraction of the US, and was far less relevant than a major country's capital. But it was, nonetheless, the state I was living in, and my ignorance towards my own country became obvious (87).

It was at this point, or soon after, that I realized that it wasn't that America was the *only* ignorant place in the whole world and everybody else was ever-knowing and completely understanding. I realized that ignorance exists in every culture but manifests itself in different ways. I finally saw that people know mostly only what is relevant to their own lives, and the fact that I was lucky enough to be a part of multiple cultures has given me a perspective and understanding that is rare. This understanding led me to another, perhaps more important realization: The people I meet throughout my life can benefit from my experience, and as a TCK it is my responsibility to *share* my stories.

Moving between various cultures, and gaining an understanding from each, leads to another main issue Pollock and Reken address, the TCK sense of cultural identity. They divide cultural identity into four main categories: foreigner, mirror, adopted, and hidden immigrant (52). The descriptions of the foreigner and the hidden immigrant I found especially relevant to the lifestyles I have been a part of. In Hong Kong, I exhibited the characteristics of a foreigner: I looked different, and I thought differently (in a cultural sense). Yet when I moved back to the US, I became a hidden immigrant; I looked the same yet had completely different worldviews. Pollock and Reken discuss the complexity a hidden immigrant faces as a foreigner in another culture, and as a foreigner in a different sense in their own when they are confronted with blending in and trying to set themselves apart (94–95).

According to Pollock and Reken, foreigners feel a sense of obligation to blend in and become a part of their new culture. I experienced this when I became apart of the international subculture of Hong Kong. Having been strongly influenced during its time as a British colony, the majority of English writing and speaking found in Hong Kong is British. Not really intending to, I developed a British accent, began referring to trash as "rubbish," erasers as "rubbers," lines as "queues," and so on. Because of my swift change of environments, I had become what Pollock and Reken like to call a "cultural chameleon," and blended into my surroundings (95). While this developed my adaptability to change, it created a challenge for me coming back to my home culture.

When I came back to the states, like many TCKs, everyone seemed to me to be the same. Everyone wore this, everyone listened to that, and everyone wants to drive this car and watch that TV show. I felt that it so greatly contradicted the eclectic lifestyle I was accustomed to, and the fact that I looked and pretty much talked like these people that seemed so mundane to me was all the more frustrating and upsetting. I felt like I *had* to stand out, and prove to everyone that I was different and that I wasn't like *them*. Pollock and Reken define these types of feelings as an "anti-identity": an inadvertent attempt by "hidden immigrants" to preserve what they view as their "true identity" (97). I look back now and see that I was trying so hard to be different that I wasn't really preserving who I really was. Trying so desperately to separate myself led to only more frustration with trying to come to terms with my cultural identity— American, Chinese, International, or some strange combination of the three. I abandoned my "anti-identity" when I finally came to terms with the fact that I wasn't just one, I was all three.

Behind the desire to acquire an "anti-identity" lies a great, often unrealized characteristic of TCKs that often leads to frustration and angst: their *arrogance*. Pollock reflects,

> It seems the very awareness which helps TCKs view a situation from multiple perspectives can also make TCKs impatient or arrogant with others who only see things from their own perspective—particularly people from their own culture. (103)

This arrogance occurs unknowingly for a number of reasons, most importantly being that often TCKs don't realize the value of their experience and how much it has actually changed their perspective. TCKs often relate better to those with similar backgrounds—and all too often get together and talk about the ignorance of their native culture. One of my closest friends, for example, had just moved to Texas from Cairo for her senior year in high school. Not having wanted to leave Egypt, her bitterness towards Texas was especially strong. We would talk a lot about how difficult it was to come back "home," and the frustration in trying to be patient with ignorance was often overwhelming. She was often asked if she rode camels to school or had to wear traditional Muslim attire. These questions seemed a nuisance, as she expected everyone to be as knowledgeable about the rest of the world as she was. Ironically, my friend, like many other TCKs, unknowingly was doing the exact thing she hated having done unto her: "equating ignorance with stupidity" (104). I feel as though my arrogance was quite strong initially, but as I came to understand American culture and develop patience with people who came from different backgrounds, I became more aware of how I was acting, and almost disgusted that I had acted so condescendingly.

I can vividly remember the day we left Hong Kong. I had to force myself to choke on the resentment I had towards my parents for making me leave—to go to Texas, of all places. I couldn't believe they would do this to me. The resentment lasted for several months afterward—through my horrific first day in American public high school, through the "do you speak Japanese?"'s, and most especially through my insatiable desire to go "home." Yet now that I have graduated and can look back on my moving experience with a little more maturity than I had going in, I can confidently say that leaving for Texas when we did was the best thing my parents ever did for me. While I hated it at the time and thought that the rest of my life could never measure up to my five years in Hong Kong, and feared that I would lose my international status, I find myself more international and understanding now than I ever was before. My uncomfortable confrontation with confused loyalties, painful views of reality, and ignorance towards my home culture challenged me to become a more adaptable and wiser person. My success in dealing with these challenges has made me no less of a TCK than I was before I moved to Texas, but has become another part of me. International. Third culture kid. Chinese. And now I can finally say, American.

Works Cited

Pollock, David C., and Ruth E. Van Reken. *Third Culture Kids*. London Nicholas Brealey, 2001.

*powerful imagery- 1st sentence

Good essay relates to reader.

Personal Narrative
Sample Essay 2

WRTG 1150
Instructor: Tobin von der Nuell

> The purpose of the assignment that prompted Erma's essay was to explore an experience that changed the writer's perspective on a particular subject. The writer was asked to focus on specifics—a specific time, person, or situation. The assignment called for reflective writing that drew upon concrete examples to discuss the significance of an event or concept. In this essay, Erma links her experiences with and feelings about reading to the complexity of moving from childhood to being "grown up."

Learning to Read

ERMA SAMPSON

I can't read. Numerous times I've tried, and somehow I just can't do it. Growing up I was a marvelous reader and I was recognized for being such by most of my teachers. However, these days I will do anything to avoid it. I'd love to be cultured and educated in literacy, but my lack of interpretative skills has kept me from being much of a book worm. The discovery of *Cliffs Notes* in high school saved my life, because the idea of having to sit down for an extended length of time *reading* made me want to kill myself. However, for some reason, I still envy those that rush home to "curl up with a good book" and can truly exclaim that the book was "far better" than the movie. The desire that some people have to read is mysteriously appealing to me.

It's not that I hate books; I've loved many books I've forced myself to read. It's just the process of actually *reading* them that I can't bring myself to actually enjoy. I blame it all on my mother. I was such a spoiled little girl. With my mom, I never had to read anything. She read all of the greatest books, emphasized the most exciting parts, and even added voices to every character. My mom reading to me as a child was a seemingly brilliant idea—a surefire way of not only expanding my mind, but enhancing my own personal need for different literature in my life. Unfortunately her bedtime stories did nothing but increase my need for more of her attention, love, and readings of *Charlotte's Web*.

I didn't always have such an incredibly short attention span. When I was young, my mom would read to my brothers and me every night, and I'd pay perfect attention, especially since she would often quiz us on what had happened in the story the following night. I think she did this because she really wanted us to remember all of the little details of the story, and thus all of the little details of our childhood. And, I do; I remember every phrase Charlotte scribbled into her web about Wilbur, and I can clearly recall every stop made while touring Willy Wonka's factory. Maybe it's the fact that these books were meant to be read by and for children, and I've just had a difficult time embracing the fact that I am no longer a child. Or maybe it's because I had no knowledge of any of the literary terms that I would grow to hate for complicating my reading ventures. I don't know, but whatever *it* is, it's keeping me from experiencing the joy that is reading a "grown-up" book, and liking it.

My mom is not the only one to blame here. If it weren't for Mr. Epstein, I'd never even have such thirst for reading. When I passed his class junior year with flying colors, despite its reputation of being brutal, he encouraged me to join his AP American Literature class senior year. I hesitated for about five minutes before I notified my advisor of my new class selection. I think his personal approach to my education gave me a feeling of superiority over many of my classmates, but nonetheless I immediately regretted my decision. I was fully aware of what I had gotten myself into. I was going to have to read, and I was going to have to read a lot. This wasn't going to be some kind of "cake" class, and I wasn't going to be able to pass it without actually reading the books. I was worried, but I didn't drop the class. That damn desire to go from completely inept to completely immersed had screwed me again.

I'm intrigued when some people say that books have changed their lives. I liked *Stuart Little*, but it certainly wasn't the *book* that changed my life. It was the moment, the experience, the way my mom looked like such a rock star in my eyes, just for reading me a story. In the eighth grade, I read *The Catcher in the Rye*, and I loved it. To feel such love for a seemingly inanimate object was oddly thrilling, and I couldn't wait to feel it again. It took an additional four years for that to happen and it left me wondering why it took me so long. I read twenty-five books during my senior year, all required for the AP class, and all without the help of *Cliffs Notes*. However, I still couldn't bring myself to walk into an actual bookstore and buy a book. Some of the books in class were dreadful, like *The Sound and Fury*, because I simply did not understand it. Other books were immensely boring like *Oedipus Rex* because I couldn't make sense of why he continued to talk *after* his eyes had been gouged out. Yet, as I reminisce about all of the crap he made us read, I'm reminded of the number of books and plays that were anything but crap. *The Stranger*, *Death of a Salesman*, and *Slaughterhouse Five* have all found a place in my heart, and on my bookshelf. I found these books to be captivating and realistic in a way I never imagined a book could be. They weren't particularly "easy" books to read, but they seemed to capture me. The angst, the struggle of the human spirit, all things that I could in some way relate to. I saw myself in those books. I was Meursault with my (at times) severe emotional detachment and moral indifference. I was Willy Loman with my ability to use extreme optimism to mask my insecurities. And, I was Billy Pilgrim in that I too have often felt quite "unstuck in time."

Growing up, books opened my eyes to many of life's harshest realities, but in a very fragile and nonthreatening kind of way. *The Giving Tree* taught me about impermanence, *Are You My Mother?* taught me to hang on to *my* mother tightly, and *Tikki Tikki Tembo* forced me to see that "Erma" really wasn't that horrible a name. However, while it's quite obvious that these "grown-up" books have harsh lessons within them as well, I struggle to want to open my eyes to them. The theme of the vast majority of my readings in high school has ultimately been tragedy and heartache. *Equus*, *Hamlet*, and *Paradise Lost* were all about tormented souls and that tricky wheel of fortune, and books like *The Color Purple*, *Hiroshima*, and *Black Boy* dealt with harsh issues like slavery and war. I walked away from these books feeling selfish for the things that I had, and worried about the similarities I had with the characters or their situations. I didn't want to be like the people in the stories, although I knew inside that I was just like them. I have never been thrilled to hear that I had similar characteristics to that of someone full of despair and pain. I know I'm not alone when I say this, but these issues are all too real and far too depressing for me to actually want to hear about, let alone read about. They are important issues, and pieces in our history, but I can't honestly say that I want to know about it. I don't like to feel sad and I certainly don't enjoy re-evaluating my entire life upon the finishing of a novel.

All those years of being taught how to read and interpret what is being read did absolutely nothing to prepare me for the kind of reading I'd be doing here at college. All of my literary self-doubt returned upon my arrival at CU. I was never really taught how to read factual texts, including textbooks, and rarely did so in high school. Simply put, I'd rather be reading fairy tales. Unfortunately life isn't a fairy tale, and I'm a business major, so I'm stuck reading about domestic spending and worker productivity. I hate reading about current events (it's horrible I know) and thus, it takes me approximately three hours to read about fourteen pages of nonfiction with any chance of retention. Those three hours are added to the previous weeks' three hours and are kept in a section of my brain marked: "Reasons why reading totally sucks." Unfortunately that section of my brain has significantly outweighed all others for the past six months, almost diminishing all hope for the revival of my reading career.

So, as is fairly obvious, I am torn between my love of books and my dislike of reading. It's quite annoying to be so on the fence about something that so many people list as a hobby. Sometimes I'll see my roommate reading on her bed and I yearn to ask her what the secret to success with reading is. Perhaps I'm chasing something that is never going to be for me. It sounds ridiculous, my longing for a used book collection, but I could never fully explain why I need this in my life. More than any reason I could ever come up with, I need this desire fulfilled to hold on to my mother for a little bit longer. I would give anything to feel the same sadness I felt when Jack the dog in *Little House on the Prairie* went missing. I'm saddened when I think about how simple life used to be. So simple that the idea of four grandparents sleeping in the same bed—from *Charlie and the Chocolate Factory* of course—had me rolling on the floor in laughter, instead of contemplating how disturbing that notion could be. I hate that I can never get lost in a story again. I'll always question the validity of the tale and I'll forget to enjoy it. I hate that life's complexities have influenced me so greatly, and I've been sucked into a hole of eternal realism. I hate that I let them.

I tried reading *East of Eden* as a part of Oprah's book club, but I quit after the second chapter. Another failed attempt. Unfortunately I no longer have any excuses. I'm not in Mr. Epstein's class anymore, so he can't really be blamed. I've forgotten what most of those literary terms mean anyway. My mom stopped reading to me years ago, so I can't really fault her any longer. She stopped for a good reason—I wasn't a baby anymore, nor am I now. I've just got to grow up, and face the music: Reading just doesn't take me away, as I don't feel safe in a make-believe world anymore. The make-believe world of today has become all too realistic.

Life in all of its pain and glory has forever taken me away from a place where salvation could be found in a book. The world is unkind, and I've wasted huge chunks of my life trying to come to terms with that. The desire to read eludes me because of its simplicity. The books have grown more complex, and the plots more real. These past few years, I witnessed myself changing—not only from a child to an adult, but from an optimist to a realist. I've been afraid of my realism, because it has opened my eyes to a whole new world of hurt and cruelty. But, it's taken me until now to see that the world is also filled with forgiveness and love, and I've sheltered myself so intensely that I've failed to notice it. So, I think I'm finally ready to embrace my realistic view of the world. As I look to my bookshelf I notice that my copy of *East of Eden* sits right next to *Charlotte's Web*. My childhood and adulthood paired off, and Steinbeck's big words are slowly overpowering poor Wilbur and essentially, my youth. I've had a death grip on my childhood ever since I realized that it could end before I wanted it to. But maybe, like my mom, these books will wait for me to grow up. Maybe the only way to learn how to read is to learn how to grow up.

Personal Narrative
Sample Essay 3

[handwritten: ★ descriptive.]
[handwritten: ★ simple question— big topic!]
[handwritten: ★ IMAGERY!]

WRTG 1150
Instructor: Tobin von der Nuell

In this richly descriptive essay, Russell reflects on a question he's asked about his girlfriend. By giving us details that appeal to our senses—sight, smell, sound, and touch—he not only tells us about what drew him to Jenny, but he also shows us pictures of important moments. Russell's use of language allows us to enter into his experience and understand its significance.

Finding Pretty

RUSSELL FOX

It was a glorious afternoon. The grass on the field was short and crisp, and the fragrance from the recent cutting still lingered in the early June breeze. I was coaching Little League baseball, adjusting the fourth graders' bat grips and stances at the plate before they were called to the infield to meet their arriving parents. Ben waited. He was the most gifted athlete on the team; he had hand-eye coordination more acute than most high school players and a fearless desire to improve. I assumed he wanted help hitting the ball farther, and I was preparing to tell him that the only possible way for him to do that would be to wait to get bigger. Instead, he stood in front of me and asked, "Russ, do you have a girlfriend?" All the fourth-grade boys would ask that question, and when I would tell them yes, they would "aw" or smirk, then laugh at my lack of knowledge of how dangerous of a situation I was in. Ben nodded, no giggling or awing, and simply asked another question: "Is she pretty to you?"

I don't know what answer I gave Ben, because I didn't know how to answer him. *Is she pretty to you?*; what does that mean? He may have wanted to know what she looked like, and if she was attractive, or if she was nice and kind and gentle; or maybe if I liked her, if I loved her, and how much, and simply didn't know how to ask. The truth is I still don't know what it is Ben wanted, but his question has been the most profound thing ever asked or said to me.

The first time I saw Jenny I was a sophomore in high school. She was the little blond sitting in the front row so close to the board that she could see her reflection in Mr. Myers's glasses. I sat in back talking with all the other boys who didn't do their homework. The back row turned test day into a community effort of shuffling papers and writing so un-identifiably in an effort to make our tests impossible to read. Jenny wasn't like me; she mastered all her work, aced every test, always perched in the front.

It wasn't until two years later that I first met Jenny. She was shoved in the back seat of a beat-up Explorer with me and three of my friends who dragged Jenny along with us after their volleyball game. It was December and we raced through Niwot blaring music with our windows rolled down, freezing our cheeks and yelling whatever lyrics we could make out through the crackle of the speakers. The night cold was pouring into the back seat, and the wind whipped around and tangled the girls' hair in their faces. It may have been the cold, or because she was being pushed, but she spent the ride leaning up against me.

I could have answered Ben's question then. Jenny was 5'10" and skinny. Her hair was blond with even lighter streaks from a summer on the Florida beaches, and her skin was smooth against my arm. That night I could have told Ben, yes, she is gorgeous. She sent lightning through my veins.

Between fall cross-country season and spring track, the early winter afternoons of my senior year consisted of leaning against a car in the parking lot, with friends, talking about girls and college. The snow melted off the lot and always kept our shoes damp as we stood flowing across the lot in thin sheets of cold evaporating water. Eventually, when we'd get too cold to stand outside, we would drive to the Phillips on the corner of the only two roads in our town. The clerk, a Chinese-American woman who didn't speak English well, always offered us advice on what number scratch ticket was the lucky card that day. We would blow twenty bucks on number five, or number two, scratching and losing, happy our feet were drying. Sweeping the shimmering scratched dust from all of our cards into a pile, we sat content. We didn't play to win money. We played because under the shimmering surface was something unknown; we played to guess at what we couldn't know, and if right, rewarded to buy more tickets, and then guess some more. We would sit at that dusty table all afternoon, and when our money ran out we sat sipping our sodas, watching the afternoon grow old.

On the days when we didn't make a trip down to the station and the sun dragged across the sky low and late in the afternoon, I asked Jenny to come and spend those short hours with me.

It was my cats that attracted her. Nine kittens, covered in silk fluff so thick that they looked round. The gray ones were her favorites; there were two, stuck somewhere between speckled and striped. She would tuck four or five kittens in her coat, and carry them around talking to them, she said protecting them from the cold of the dusty barn. Jenny and I would sit out in the barn, just talking; most of the time I talked at her, she nodded and listened and pet the kittens. What I said didn't matter; she was sitting there, listening. I would ask her questions, trying to scratch away the shimmer that concealed her; sometimes she'd answer me, sometimes not and just look up and smile with her eyes that burned sharp and bright. Dust, hay, grain, and old wood filled the air that smelled warm, despite the cold of the Colorado winter. Much of the barn was covered in thin dust expelled from the hundreds of bails of hay. The kittens and the wood all were dirty, and you could see little paw prints on the saddles layered in dust. You could see across the cart cover where they would slip and swipe clean the leather. The barn was a safe place for me to go on the frigid afternoons; the chickens and the horses all wandered. Nothing they did was in order, yet it all was natural and all made sense. I felt that same way about Jenny, too. I didn't understand her; she was too rich and colorful to be understood. I was just happy there in the barn with her.

She kissed me one day after coming from the barn. By her car, she simply kissed me and said, "Have a good day Mr. Fox!" in her flirtatious, cute manner. Turning abruptly, leaving a swirl in the gravel driveway, she got in her car and drove off.

In the spring we took salsa classes, and I taught her swing. The speed and swing and jazz camouflage intimacy. Spinning through a crowd of others, dragging swirls across the floor with our feet, she taught me to lead with clarity, and she trusted my every step. The trumpet and saxophone's soulful notes mixed with the swirling air from the fans and the sweat beads on the forehead of the dancers. The air hops with life that cannot be duplicated with a song or a dance, but only with the exact passion of song, dance, and trust. I loved those nights with Jenny. A time to immerse ourselves in a room full of people, and a time to be close and intimate.

As my infatuation with Jenny formed to love, so did my impression of Ben's question. Jenny was much more than beautiful. The heat of a July night would force us to spend evenings and nights down at the lake by her house. The lake was small, but deep and cool. We would swim out to the floating dock in the middle, her long arms slicing the black water, letting long smooth ripples flow behind her. I would pad-dle and pant, scratch and claw my way after her, dragging my vertical body through layers of cold water that she seemingly glided over. We would lie on the dock surrounded by the black water and gray trees on the bank; I would pant and she would laugh, and lay her head on my damp shoulder, and listen to my pounding breath. Some nights we would sit on the bank, drink beers, and talk about everything. Her ar-ticulate ideas and beliefs would force my own to slowly accept others. Those summer nights, when our words would mix with the buzz of mosquitoes and crickets, she taught me how to be kind, how to laugh.

Waking up in the middle of my summer trip with her, when the out-side air was still chilled, seeping up off the river surface, Jenny would squirm in her down bag, bring herself up on her knees in her burnt red cocoon, and peer at me. She'd burst out, "It's too cold! Malo..." then she'd flip around the tiny tent, rolling over me and the bags tucked in the corner. She'd stop to ask if I was too cold as well, and I'd laugh when she'd continue her rolling routine, shaking the tent feverously, calling out, "You're a crazy, too cold, you're a crazy." Jenny's passion for life flowed in her voice. There were times when she'd sit next to me and talk in French with the elegance of a native. When she was done with her idea, she'd sit and look at me, waiting for a response, knowing full well that not a single word had registered with me. Other times she would insert an English word, and highlight it, so within a twenty-second French spat, she would give you two words that didn't mean anything without their French context. Her games made me squirm in anticipation just as she did avoiding the cold.

Whenever I'd turn the spotlight to her, she would dismiss her flawless GPA and refuse to acknowledge that she was one of the top volleyball players in the nation. She'd look at me and say, "Don't be silly, Rus-sell, you're making it all up," while a stack of scholarship offers sat behind her. Yet with all her games and all her play, her elegance and intelligence would command attention that hid in the beauty of her voice. I don't understand her reluctance to take credit for her achieve-ments, but through her reluctance I began to notice my attempts to draw attention to mine.

I have tried to answer Ben's question hundreds of times. *Is she pretty to you?* The question is powerful because it can't be answered with a sentence or idea. Beauty is held in uncertainty, emotion is muffled in clarity. The un-timed rhythm of the barn animals, the mix of sweat and jazz in the dance hall, the speckled gray of the cat, and the ripples in the summer lake all lack order. But they capture the beauty of our unstable world. This beauty is found in the cracks of life, the time not documented.

Summer beauty is not the child running down the dock and jumping into the lake. *Pretty* is the thud...thud...thud...of his feet stomping the wooden planks, the gasp of air as he tucks his knees, the moment before he crashes into the shimmering water, exploding the uniform ripples into a passionate dance. Jenny is that space between the cracks of my life.

I wish I could answer Ben again. I would tell him that his question was beautiful, and then I would tell him that I love her, that I love her so very much. He wouldn't understand, not at eight; but later, when he falls in love, confused and content, he might.

Analysis
Sample Essay 1

WRTG 1150
Instructor: Lonni Pearce

> In this essay, Lena responds to an assignment that asked her to analyze
> a significant theme or concept in a short text. By using concrete details
> from the text and relating them to the "bigger picture" of the social con-
> text out of which Alice Walker's story was written, Lena articulates her
> interpretation of what is significant and important in Walker's story.

Path to Heritage

LENA KANG

Alice Walker's "Everyday Use" focuses on the cultural struggles faced by many African-Americans during a significantly chang-ing time in history—the Civil Rights Movement. Individuals were unsure of how to incorporate their traditional African heritage and fam-ily traditions into their daily lives. Such is the basis for Walker's short story; "Everyday Use" explores this difficult concept by means of a simple family who is connected yet distanced from one another. Mama is the hard-working head of the household who is unsure of how to deal with her daughters; Dee is the haughty older daughter who is unable to iden-tify with her family in many ways; Maggie is the timid younger daughter who is afraid to stand up to her sister, Dee. Throughout the course of the story, Walker identifies the characters with many aspects of the Civil Rights Movement. Walker is able to capture this struggle in her writing with distinct characterization of the three main characters and a domi-nant theme of heritage.

Walker gives Mama, Maggie, and Dee (Wangero) well-defined person-alities in order to illustrate the various attitudes of African-Americans during the Civil Rights period. Mama is described as "a large, big-boned woman with rough, man-working hands" who wants to gain approval from Dee and give acceptance to Maggie (75). She makes a reference to how she sometimes dreams her life is like one on a TV show. She would be "a hundred pounds lighter, [her] skin like an uncooked barley pan-cake[...]" (75). This is because Dee is a superficial person and is always criticizing her family for looking ragged and poor. Walker also allows the reader to see Mama's acceptance of Maggie. In the beginning of the story, Mama describes Maggie as "a lame animal, perhaps a dog run over by some careless person rich enough to own a car, [who] sidles up to someone who is ignorant enough to be kind[...]" (75). In the end of the story, however, Mama takes Maggie's defense when Dee tries to steal the quilts and then sits in the company of Maggie until the sun goes down.

Much like the situation in the story, the characterization of Mama is typical to many "colored" people during this difficult time. Like Mama, the "colored" people wanted to be accepted by the whites, but were unsure of what to do in order to gain that acceptance. When Mama is talking about the TV show she dreams of, she mentions how "Johnny Carson has much to do to keep up with [her] quick and witty tongue," but then she says "who ever knew a Johnson with a quick tongue? Who can even imagine me looking a strange white man in the eye?" (75). Mama realizes that although she does want to be on an equal level with the white people, she, as an individual, feels unable to find a way to receive the acceptance she craves. In addition, the tensions caused by the Civil Rights Movement made such communication between the white and black people very difficult due to extreme amounts of racism and hatred.

On the contrary, Maggie plays a very passive role in the story. Maggie is self-conscious due to "the burn scars down her arms and legs" and difficulty in learning (74). She feels inferior to her "accomplished" older sister, Dee, who "has held life always in the palm of one hand" (74). Near the end of "Everyday Use," Dee asks Mama for some family quilts that had been saved for Maggie. When Mama objects, Maggie says, "She can have them, Mama.... I can 'member Grandma Dee without the quilts." Even when Dee attempts to take the quilts that mean the world to her, Maggie remains quiet and allows her sister to do as she pleases. This quote also shows the strength that Maggie does have. Even though she is viewed as the lesser of the two sisters, she does not feel the need to hold on to material possessions in order to remember her heritage.

Maggie's character symbolizes another large group of African-Americans during the Civil Rights Movement: those who were too afraid and ashamed to demand equal rights from those they found superior—the white people. Like Maggie, many of the black people had been so oppressed and belittled over the period of their lives that they felt physically and psychologically inferior to the white race. Because of these feelings of complete mediocrity, this particular group found it very difficult to find their place in the Movement. They were too afraid to openly object their position in society even though they knew it was wrong and wanted a change.

On the contrary, the character of Dee exemplifies yet another group of African-Americans. Dee is educated, witty, and action-oriented, which proves to be overpowering when compared to the personalities of

Mama and Maggie. Such is the case when Dee comes to visit her family. Dee proceeds to take everything that she wants even though she knows that her mother and sister cherish the items, like the butter churn that has been in the family for so many generations that "you could see where thumbs and fingers had sunk into the wood" (80). The butter churn symbolizes the traditions of Dee's family. This particular item has been passed down through so many generations of their family that the indents from their fingers are permanently imprinted into the grooves of the wood.

Dee's character more closely identifies with the particular group of people who were very active in their demands for equal rights. People like Dee were at the forefront of the Civil Rights Movement and were the ones who most loudly voiced their objection to the mistreatment of African-Americans in the United States. This particular group led the way for people who were more like Mama and Maggie because the more timid people weren't willing to jeopardize the few freedoms they had gained for the purpose of complete equality. Without the leadership and sacrifice of people like Dee, the concerns of African-Americans across the country may never have been heard.

Although Walker has many themes in her short story, the theme of heritage is the most obvious. The story in its entirety is a parallel to the process of discovering one's background. Dee most outwardly exhibits her newly discovered African heritage by changing her name to Wangero in order to be free of the name the "people who oppress" gave to her (78). She then decides that she wants many of the items that signify her family's history and culture—the butter churn and the family quilts. Dee believes that by changing her name and owning those items, she will be better able to identify with her past. In contrast, Mama learns about her heritage in a much more subtle way. It isn't until Dee attempts to acquire the quilts that Mama had been saving for Maggie that she fully understands the great deal of culture she and Maggie have. Mama realizes that "it was Grandma Dee and Big Dee who taught [Maggie] how to quilt herself" (81). Mama recognizes that all along, Maggie has been the one who has helped to hold on to their traditions by learning the family tradition of quilting from her grandmother. Mama, unlike Dee, lives the simple, traditional life her family has always lived rather than modernizing. In this she is holding on to traditions that are a part of her family heritage.

Alice Walker's "Everyday Use" embodies the significance of the Civil Rights Movement and family tradition by using distinct characters and themes. The struggle during the Civil Rights Movement is often difficult to grasp, especially on the level of individuals. Unless a person actually lived during that time, it is almost impossible to understand the conflicts at the time. Walker's short story gives the reader a small taste of these struggles in a family setting. People can more easily relate to family hardships, so Walker connects these simpler issues to the much larger issue of Civil Rights.

Analysis
Sample Essay 2

WRTG 1250
Instructor: Frances Charteris

Good analytical writing shows readers how texts are constructed and why the texts are significant. In this case, the "texts" are photographs—Lindsay describes both how ParkeHarrison uses the medium of photography and why his photographs carry such power. To see the photographs Lindsay discusses, see the George Eastman House Museum's website at http://www.geh.org/parkeharrison/index.htm.

Tidying Nature: Everyman's Quest in the Photography of Robert ParkeHarrison

LINDSAY LOWE

Photographer Robert ParkeHarrison stars in his own pieces as a balding, shuffling mortal given the colossal task of reining in nature. This Everyman marches through a host of sepia landscapes, armed only with a ladder and a few daVincian contraptions, and tries his best to take charge of impossibly vast terrains. These tasks all seem too big for him, but the viewer, who relates to his human need to make nature manageable, understands why he takes this mending, this tidying, upon himself. In almost all ParkeHarrison's pieces, Everyman is trying not only to manage nature, but also to fix some part of it. In nearly all his works, ParkeHarrison comments on the damage humans have inflicted on the earth, and on what a massive task it will be to repair what we have destroyed.

Everyman is nothing if not creative. In each photograph, he finds a more bizarre, inventive way of tending to the earth. He kneels over a fissure in the Earth's surface, patiently stitching it back together with a needle taller than he is, attempts to clean a polluted cloud with a rag and bucket. Most modern photographers would rely on digital editing to assemble these whimsical settings; ParkeHarrison, however, prefers traditional methods. He borrows images from a variety of sources, and then, cutting and pasting paper negatives, collages them with his own photographs to construct a single cohesive image (Flagan, par. 2). To remove flaws and blemishes, he washes this assembled piece in several layers of monochromatic paint, accounting for the brown or bluish tints to many of his pieces (Flagan, par. 2). Even after this process, small irregularities remain, giving his images the air of antique, decaying photographs. Far from detracting from the pictures, this impression of age lends a certain haunting nostalgia to his pieces; today's viewer, caught up in an age of greed and fast-paced technology, thinks wistfully of the days when one human could innocently set out to mend the world.

ParkeHarrison once said of his work, "I want there to be a combination of the past juxtaposed with the modern" (ParkeHarrison). He accomplishes this by tinting very modern subject matter with the sepia finish we associate with more wholesome, simple times. He embraces this kind of old-fashioned innocence in several of his pieces, placing an almost childlike trust in Everyman's ability to restore what we have destroyed in nature. *Passage*, one of these more optimistic works, depicts Everyman building a wooden bridge across an expanse of water, using only a small hammer to nail the planks together. It is an absurdly difficult task, but Everyman, in true form, makes do. The section of finished bridge fills the lower right side of the frame, revealing his progress. A small, barely visible point of land hovers in the upper left-hand corner, suggesting that Everyman's persistence will soon pay off. To further convince the viewer of Everyman's imminent triumph, ParkeHarrison guides the viewer's eye along one line from the bridge to the strip of earth, suggesting that the bridge will inevitably lead to land. In this work, ParkeHarrison places a great deal of confidence in human resolve and potential. Though Everyman is not directly repairing nature in this piece, his successful bridge-building represents humans' ability to meet seemingly impossible challenges. ParkeHarrison celebrates this human capacity to overcome insurmountable tasks in several other works, such as *Clearing*, which depicts Everyman sweeping thousands of tons of rubbish into a pile with a garden rake, and *Navigator*, in which Everyman climbs above the clouds with a hand-made wooden ladder.

Though a faith in human determination runs through several of ParkeHarrison's pieces, it does not extend to all. In some works, such as *Breathing Machine* and *Guardian*, he takes a grimmer view of the human condition. In *Breathing Machine*, Everyman lies face-up in a pool of dingy, polluted water, his head almost entirely submerged. Noxious smoke billows from the distant outline of an industrial plant. No one could survive long in this poisonous environment, but Everyman, always resourceful, has built an elaborate breathing device, which he holds on his stomach and operates with a wooden crank. A tube extends from his mouth to a glass box containing a single oak leaf. One of ParkeHarrison's most frightening images, *Breathing Machine* presents a scenario in which we have replaced all fertile life with smog-spewing factories. To survive in this hostile world, Everyman must cling on to the one piece of nature that remains: a single leaf. This photograph treats humans' relationship with nature differently than works like *Clearing*, *Passage* and *Mending the Earth*; while in those images ParkeHarrison celebrates a human capacity to repair the damaged earth, in *Breathing Machine* he reminds us of our complete dependence on nature. We may have resolve and potential, but without nature we will die.

In some cases, ParkeHarrison even questions this potential. He depicts a brown, barren expanse of tree stumps and dry branches. The landscape is not entirely dead; two slender stems shoot up from a stump, reaching high enough to spread a small arc of tangled branches over the other stumps. It is atop this spindly growth that Everyman perches, poised to protect this last remnant of life in this otherwise barren environment. Rather than seeming noble, his fierce loyalty to the frail tree seems pathetic, for it is only a matter of time before this feeble growth will join the dead branches layering the ground. One feels terribly sorry for Everyman, knowing his cause to be useless. In this piece, ParkeHarrison seems to despair over humans' attempts to protect nature, implying that Everyman has come too late to make a real change. Still, he seems to respect Everyman's efforts. Observing Everyman's outstretched arms and joined feet, the Crucifixion comes to mind. If this allusion was intentional, it suggests that Everyman's gifts to the environment have not been in vain; perhaps some good may come of his sacrifices.

A respect for Everyman's labors lies at the core of each of ParkeHarrison's photographs. Though ParkeHarrison often despairs at the futility of Everyman's efforts, his images never suggest that Everyman should stop trying. Even in his bleakest, most discouraging pieces, ParkeHarrison commends Everyman's tenacity. This tenacity, in fact, links him to Everyman; after viewing the photographs, one comes away not only appreciating Everyman's resolve, but also admiring the artist's dedication. ParkeHarrison's willingness to meticulously construct each setting and image mirrors Everyman's firm determination to mend nature. The images themselves often present bleak scenarios, but ParkeHarrison's steady devotion to his craft shines through each work. Ultimately, we respect ParkeHarrison for his labors, hoping some of his resolve will rub off on us as we embark on one of our most daunting missions: mending the destroyed Earth.

Works Cited

Flagan, Are. "Apotheosis–Grapevine–Robert ParkeHarrison." FindArticles. March 2002. FindArticles. 12 February 2006. <http://www. findarticles.com/p/articles/mi_m2479/is_5_29/ai_84841842>

ParkeHarrison, Robert. *The Architect's Brother*. No date. Twin Palms Twelvetrees Press. 14 Feb. 2006. <http://www.twinpalms.com/ ?p=backlist&bookID=82>.

Inquiry
Sample Essay 1

WRTG 1150
Instructor: Daniel Brigham

An inquiry essay begins with a good question. In her investigation of why many people enjoy horror films and haunted houses, Kelsey asks a question that not only is personally interesting to her but is also of interest to other people. By drawing on the work of scholars from a variety of fields, Kelsey looks at several explanations for people's enjoyment of the horrific. She then compares the scholarly explanations with her own experience, weaving together the academic and personal as she researches this popular cultural phenomenon.

Happily Horrified

KELSEY McDONALD

"You may enter." The knobbly, cracked hand of the hooded speaker sweeps slowly across his body and comes to rest upon the arched doors. For a moment, all are silent; his eyes laugh menacingly at ours. Then, he pushes, and the solid oak doors creak open. I suck in my breath; I can hear my blood pulsating in my ears. The hand pulling mine gently leads me into the black uncertainty. As my eyes gradually adjust, I see that I am following my friends' figures down a long corridor, our shadows drifting silently along the peeling walls. My eyes fall upon the silhouette of a young girl floating in a pool of light at the end of the hallway. We creep forward; one foot, then the next. Suddenly, the pool of light is enveloped by blackness. We stop: a noise behind us. I spin around. The girl is now standing where we had just been a half minute before. Her long, black hair clings to her cheeks as she lifts her head. I start pushing. "Run! Just go!"

I sprint down the hall, through a bathroom smeared with sanguine blood. I shove my way through frigid, hanging corpses, past cackling clowns with knives held high in their clenched fists. Finally, an empty room; I slow. My heavy breath hangs in the air, and a bead of cold sweat trickles down through my hair.

Now where? The lights are dimming, the walls seeming to cave in. Then, the roar of a starting chainsaw. Again my legs, though I can't feel them, are carrying me faster and faster. The roar overpowers my eardrums, then grows softer, more distant.

Finally, I'm back in the cold night air. My hands hit my knees, my chest heaves. My best friend Kati is beside me now. The rest of our group appears, laughing hysterically.

"I didn't know you guys could run so fast," Chris manages between bouts of laughter.

"That was awesome!" I say, and Kati agrees.

We pile into Chris's '93 Pathfinder. As we drive back to Kati's house, the others laugh and compare favorite rooms and characters of the haunted house we just left, but I'm lost in my thoughts. *Why is that considered entertainment? What makes people want to put themselves in situations like that? I was so scared in there, but I loved it!*

It seems so paradoxical. One of the most fundamental assumptions of natural human behavior is that we avoid the repulsive and seek the pleasurable. As Noel Carroll, professor and author of fifteen books and hundreds of articles on philosophical subjects, so eloquently points out, "We do not, for example, attempt to add some pleasure to a boring afternoon by opening the lid of a steamy trash can in order to savor its unwholesome stew of broken bits of meat, moldering fruits and vegetables, and noxious, unrecognizable clumps" (275). So how can it be that, in the case of horror films and haunted houses, not only do we seek the revolting, but we find pleasure in it?

The human species has historically always acknowledged that the world is full of "dark" and "evil" aspects ("Horror Story" 245). Beyond this simple acknowledgement, however, humans have always maintained a *fascination* for the "other-worldly." The ancient Egyptians are remembered today for their preoccupation with the realm of the spirits and their diligent earthly work that would prepare them for what they believed would follow death; ancestor worship began with the Zhou Dynasty in China in 1500 B.C.; classical mythology depicts characters such as Medusa (who turned onlookers to stone and brandished a scalp of snakes), the Hydra (a many-headed water beast who acted as guardian of the Underworld), and the Cyclops (a one-eyed giant). Many of these tales involved a hero (for example, Orpheus or Heracles), who was driven to journey through the land of the dead in order to accomplish his mission or reach his destination (Wilson).

The modern horror genre, however, began its development in the late eighteenth century. As the Enlightenment Movement continued to find scientific explanations for seemingly every aspect of life, many fought against this "rational, ordered world" with tales of terror, now known as "Gothic" literature. These stories related heinous evils and were often framed against an ominous medieval backdrop. This history may offer insight into another reason the horror genre remains popular today. Science and technology continue to define and shape our world in an increasingly ordered and deliberate fashion. It is possible that many find the impossibilities of the horror genre as an outlet for rebellion against today's scientific, classified, formulized universe. To be sure, however, the legacy of Gothic literature continues to awe and entice hordes of indulgers to the present day, and will inevitably continue to do so, as the human fascination with and curiosity towards evil has not waned ("Horror Story" 245).

Perhaps much of our fascination is a result of the religious framework that seems to inevitably encompass the horror genre. In almost every religion there is an ongoing battle between the epitome of good and the ultimate evil. I believe we are intrigued by these ultimate forms of evil, the work of Satan and demons, unknown magical forces. These films and simulations represent, for most people, their greatest fears. Viewers and participants are often required to confront death, and perhaps even what may follow death, and the greatest forces of evil imaginable to the human mind. Through the atrocities that horror films and even haunted houses offer to us, we must necessarily explore religious themes and essentially our personal beliefs and views on the struggle of good versus evil. And because these situations are only simulations, we are able to leave the situation with the sense that we triumphed over that evil.

Our fascination may also result from the impossibility of what we are offered through horrifying simulations. Senior lecturer in Moral Philosophy at the Scottish University of St. Andrews, Berys Gaut, claims in his "The Paradox of Horror" that because monsters are "physically impossible according to our conceptual scheme, we are [...] curious about them, and find them fascinating" (296). Carroll agrees, expressing his belief that because monsters are so unusual to us and to our cultural understanding, we have a natural desire to learn about them (281). Take, for example, the monster in Lovecraft's "The Dunwich Horror":

> Bigger'n a barn...all made o' squirmin ropes...hull thing sort o' shaped like a hen's egg bigger'n anything, with dozen o' legs like hogsheads that haff shut up when they step...nothin' solid abaout it—all like jelly...great bulgin' eyes all over it...ten or twenty maouths or trunks astickn' aout all along the sides... (Carroll 281)

However, Gaut also points out that "not all horror fictions involve monsters," that an extremely prominent and popular subcategory of horror is the depiction of the serial killer (296). In the 2007 thriller *Disturbia*, actor Shia LaBeouf, through his teenage character Kale Brecht, demonstrates the natural human inquisitiveness inspired not by a "monster," but by such a "slasher."

Under house arrest for "popping" his Spanish teacher, and lacking the TV, Internet, and gaming services (which his mother had promptly aborted following his incarceration), Kale is left with nothing better to occupy his time than building Twinkie towers and spying on the unsuspecting residents of his wealthy suburban neighborhood. Kale learns that the suspect in an abducted woman's investigation (a case similar to several homicides in a nearby town) is thought to have been driving a blue 1967 Ford Mustang with a dented front left fender. Kale later observes his neighbor, Robert Turner, pushing just such a car, dented front left fender and all, into Turner's garage. Kale informs his friends, Ronnie and Ashley, of what he had discovered, and they all decide to "stakeout," keeping both binoculars and a video recorder trained on Turner's house. Later that night, the trio spots a frantic woman racing hysterically through Turner's hallways and rooms, while through the curtains, they see Turner's silhouette brandishing a glaring, silver knife. The three lunge forward, leaning as close as possible to the glass of Kale's bedroom window, straining to see what will happen. Their rapid, heavy breathing fogs the window; their large, frightened eyes dart from woman to Turner (*Disturbia*). All three are visibly petrified, but none can tear their eyes from the sight. Their fascination of the scene has glued them to the sight of it, despite their fear. As Carroll suggests, "One wants to gaze upon the unusual even when it is simultaneously repelling" (286).

So we see that, through the fascination, we can still feel fear. But through the fear, can we also feel pleasure? Some researchers believe no. These proponents of the "aftermath model" assert that the observer does not, in fact, enjoy the fearful experience (the haunted house or horror film) itself, but rather the relief at the resolution of the experience, when the brain finally relaxes after its tensed, stressful state. As the University of California at Los Angeles assistant research psychologist Raphael Rose stated, "There is a profound sense of relief when the terror ends," and it is for this immense release that so many endure the fear and displeasure of, say, a horror film or haunted house (Pressley).

The flaw, here, is the aftermath model's underlying assumption that positive emotions can only occur *after* the fearful stimulus has gone; that the human species can only experience one emotion at a time.

I know different. As the dramatic music resonates in my ears, my anticipation heightens. I'm certain something big is about to happen. Actress
Julia Stiles, as mother Katherine Thorn in the 2006 film *The Omen*, is
staring questioningly at her reflection in the mirror. Then, there it is!
The haunting reflection of a red-eyed demon breathing down her neck! I
jump about a foot in the air. I pull my eyes away to turn and look at Col-
leen, sitting next to me on the couch. My jaw hangs agape in shock and
fright, yet my lips are turned up at the corners in an excited smile; I'm
terrified, and I'm having a great time!

This cannot be, according to the aftermath model, but is in direct con-
cordance with the theory of "co-activation." Andrade and Cohen believe
that individuals are in fact capable of experiencing positive feelings in
addition to fear, and all at the same time. These researchers analyzed
the responses of seventy-five students from the University of California
at Berkeley to a frightening stimulus. Each student first observed two
minutes of a documentary (to standardize emotional levels), followed by
four and a half minutes of a horror movie. The participants were asked
to report their levels of happy and fearful emotions, and if and when they
experienced these emotions simultaneously, at intervals throughout the
film. From the study, Andrade and Cohen concluded that not only did
participants feel both fear and pleasure at the same time, but that the
more fear they felt, the more pleasure they experienced as well (291).

As I myself agree with Andrade and Cohen's theory, because I know that
I do in fact enjoy the scary movie or haunted house as I experience it,
I grew curious as to what my fellow University of Colorado at Boulder
students would have to say on the subject. And so, I decided to conduct
a study of my own. I polled twenty CU–Boulder students who claimed to
enjoy horror films and/or haunted houses. Each student was asked when
he or she found their experiences *most* pleasurable: during the experience or after the stimulus had gone. Nine of the ten males questioned
responded that they enjoyed the experience most while it was occurring,
and nine of ten females responded in the same way. Thus, it seems that
the aftermath model is inaccurate and that co-activation offers the better
explanation.

But it seems to me that "co-activation" of emotions is not so well-defined
as one might think. As Gaut suggests, "There is no pattern of physiological changes or set of sensations peculiar to each emotion, and
an emotion may be associated with different sensations…" (302). For
example, the physiological manifestations of our responses to fear are
extremely similar to that of love at first sight: sweating; muscle tension;
rapid, pounding heartbeat; difficulty breathing. Stanley Schachter, author of "The Interaction of Cognitive and Physiological Determinants of

Emotional State," proposes that excitation is not specific to pleasurable or displeasurable emotions, and that the excitation from either of these causes is the same. Therefore, when they are experienced in sequence, they add to each other. For example, if one experiences excitation from a pleasurable experience, say a funny line or scene in a horror film, the following murder attempt on the hero's life will serve to intensify the emotion the viewer had experienced in the scene before.

Can this suggestion, termed the "excitation transfer theory" by Dolf Zillman, be explained scientifically? In fact it can, by the brain's dispersion of catecholamines. These neurotransmitters are released to signal your body to respond to a stimulus, whether fearful or pleasurable. The effects of these catecholamines, however, diminish relatively slowly, and so, excitation by a previous stimulus or emotion is intensified by subsequent or simultaneously occurring emotions (Zillman). This makes it possible to "find both negative emotional responses and their objects pleasant," due to their intensification of pleasurable stimuli (Gaut 302).

I know this to be true. I always find a horror film that contains at least some comic relief to be more enjoyable. The tension is briefly broken and I am excited by a positive emotion. When the next scene cuts to a portrayal of the murderer, I am already enjoying the movie, excited and intrigued, with attention fully focused. This next scene, therefore, seems even more enjoyable than it would have been had the previous scene been excluded.

Gaut takes the excitation transfer theory one step further: He proposes that negative emotions may not be experienced at all; that while the objects (or experiences) that cause the emotions may be negative, the emotions themselves are not necessarily so. Simply because what we are witnessing may be unpleasant does not require that what we are feeling is also unpleasant (300).

These emotions can be interpreted as enjoyable, because the individual understands that what he or she is experiencing is merely a simulation. "Because we know that the monsters are only fictional, the fear and disgust they arouse in us are muted in comparison with what they would be if we were to meet such monsters in real life, which allows the pleasures of curiosity more easily to outweigh the displeasures of fear and disgust" (296). This is commonly referred to as the "control thesis": When the individual feels in control of his situation, in the case of horror films and haunted houses, he realizes that nothing will really happen to him.

Andrade and Cohen refer to this psychological security, and its resulting detachment from depicted events, as the "protective frame." In order to analyze the degree to which enjoyment was affected by the protective frame, Andrade and Cohen recruited eighty-three University of California at Berkeley students, and again asked them to watch four and a half minutes of a horror film, while reporting their levels of enjoyment at intervals throughout the clip. The procedure was then repeated with the same students, but this second time, the researchers installed within their subjects a stronger protective frame: During the horror clip, Andrade and Cohen placed pictures of the actors in their every-day clothes next to the screen, reminding the viewers that the characters were fictional (293). The results showed that enjoyment levels increased from the standardization experiment, in which no pictures of the actors were placed next to the screen. From this, we see that when people feel sufficiently disengaged and detached from the events, they can feel pleasure along with their fear (294).

It seems to me, however, that this psychological security has individually defined boundaries. I have often heard fellow horror film patrons complain that they did not enjoy a particular movie, because they did not experience sufficient fear. For these individuals, the stimulus they experienced was unable to adequately overcome the erected barrier of their protective frame, and they were therefore prevented from enjoying the arousal that is triggered in response to fear. Yet the situation also loses its pleasure if a simulation becomes too real and evokes *too much* fear.

"No way, guys! No way! I can't go in there!" Our line was at a standstill. The high black walls of the haunted house had been shrinking over the past several feet, and we now found ourselves staring down the only exit: one tiny door, about three feet high. Kati was on the floor, almost in tears; she would not, could not, convince herself that if she tried to crawl through that door, she would come out all right on the other side. For Kati, what she was being asked to do was just *too* frightening, *too* real. The experience had more than surpassed her psychological barrier, and the pleasures of curiosity or fascination, or any pleasure for that matter, were not enough to allow her to enjoy the fictional experience.

When, however, an experience strikes the perfect balance (is fearful enough to trigger emotional responses yet remains just unrealistic enough that psychological security is maintained), not only can an individual enjoy the curiosity and fascination, along with the emotional responses that are triggered by such an experience, but also a sort of mental stimulation.

The screen comes into focus. Two men lay, beaten and bruised, in an abandoned, rusted bathroom. One is chained to a pipe, while the other is similarly bound to a bathtub. Clues have been left for the men that lead them to a saw. Once the tool is discovered, however, the two quickly learn that the blade is too dull to sever the wrought-iron. It soon becomes apparent to the audience that the capturer has intentionally left the fate of each man in his own hands: Will he choose to amputate his own foot above the chain that binds him, and escape; or will he keep his appendage, but die, chained in the cement room (*Saw*)?

"Oh my gosh!" I turn to Emily. "I don't know if I could do it! What would you do?" She thinks for a while. "I'd do it," she finally replies.

Through simulations such as haunted houses and horror films, we are given the opportunity to place ourselves in a particular situation which, if real, would test every ounce of our strength, both mental and physical. But because the situation is only a representation of the actual event, we are able to question, debate, and discover how we ourselves would react. "We can have the experience without dealing with the repercussions," said a friend of mine, Tim McNerney, when discussing possible explanations for people's enjoyment of horror films. Graham Masterton, author of more than sixty horror and thriller novels, wrote that people enjoy horror because the genre

> depicts ordinary people dealing with extraordinary threats. They like to imagine, *What would I do if a dark shadow with glowing red eyes appeared in my bedroom at night? What would I do if I heard a sinister scratching inside the walls of my house? What would I do if my husband's head turned around 360 degrees?* (Hoffner and Cantor 43)

They have the opportunity to imagine how they themselves would react, how their decisions would differ from the characters', and how the outcome might therefore change. Perhaps this allows an individual to somehow feel superior to the characters by believing that his "better" decision would have allowed the monster to be defeated, the victim to be rescued, or for the story to have an all-around more satisfactory conclusion.

I have discovered, however, that while all of these theories and studies accurately describe why many people put themselves in haunting or horrifying situations, there is one particular explanation that remains the most common and most universal. I asked twenty University of Colorado at Boulder students whether they enjoyed the adrenaline rush they experienced when watching a horror film or visiting a haunted house. All twenty students (ten male and ten female) responded that yes, they did enjoy this rush *and* that this was the number-one reason why they chose to engage in such frightening experiences.

So obviously, most people have heard of, and probably experienced, an adrenaline rush. But what exactly occurs in such a response? And what makes it enjoyable?

The answers lie in our bodies' natural "fight-or-flight" response, of which epinephrine, commonly known as adrenaline, is the main ingredient. This hormone is released from the adrenal medulla, located just above our kidneys, and enters into our bloodstream. Epinephrine causes our heart rates to increase, along with our respiratory rates, our arterioles (which carry and direct blood-flow) to dilate, our muscles to tense, and "our attention to focus for quick and effective responses to threats" (Choi). The sudden increase in epinephrine levels also signals the brain to produce endorphins. These hormones, released from the pituitary gland into the bloodstream, and from the hypothalamus into the spinal cord and brain, are the body's natural painkillers. Binding to opiate receptors in the brain, they contribute to an individual's sense of well-being and happiness, and elicit feelings of euphoria. In a sense, endorphins are the body's natural drug and are responsible for a natural "high," contributing significantly to the enjoyment of the rush.

Sylvia Kriebig and a team of researchers conducted a study to determine the effects of adrenaline on emotions caused by fear. Kriebig and her team used electrodes to measure the respiratory and heart rates, and the electrodermal reactions of their subjects, in response to a "fear-inducing film." The team also videotaped the facial expressions of the subjects as the film was watched and recorded their verbal responses following the film. The subjects reported their levels of emotional intensity using a ten-point scale. This was the standardization trial. For a second viewing of the film, each subject received a supplementary injection of epinephrine. Based on all collected data, both the physiological and verbal responses, the team determined that the increased levels of epinephrine led the subjects to experience "higher intensity of emotions," both fearful and pleasurable (801). Higher intensity of both fear and pleasure means higher levels of endorphins, and so, greater enjoyment.

When the danger, or simulation of such, subsides, however, no adrenaline (or no epinephrine) is released, and begins the body's return to homeostasis (its normal functioning state). Though no research has been conducted on this point, it seems to me that, from a developmental standpoint, when this occurs, the restoration must mean that the individual has "won" his battle, overcome the obstacle, defeated the danger, which in itself is accompanied by an overwhelming sense of excitement, triumph, and pleasure.

In reality, no one theory can account for the human enjoyment of horror. In fact, our pleasure is derived from aspects of all the theories and models explored above. Each individual's enjoyment may depend on a unique combination of these explanations, and in varying proportions. Throughout this investigation process, I have come to see each of these aspects of enjoyment in my personal pursuance of horrifying experiences. I believe the fascination and curiosity are the most heavily weighted, which, due to my psychological security, I am able to solicit and relish, without fear of consequence. Yet, for others, it's all about the adrenaline; still others: the triumph.

Well, I'd better go. We're back at Kati's house, and the others have just started the movie. I'd hate to miss the beginning of *Silence of the Lambs*!

Works Cited

Carroll, Noel. "Why Horror?" *Arguing About Art*. Eds. Alex Neil and Aaron Ridley. New York: Routledge. 2nd ed. 2002. 275–93.

Choi, Charles. "Why We Love to be Scared." *Live Science*. 30 Oct 2006. 1 Nov 2007. <http://livescience.com/health/061030_fear_factor.html>.

Disturbia. DVD. Prod. Jackie Marcus, Joe Medjuck, and E. Bennett Walsh. Dir. D.J. Caruso. Dreamworks Video. 104 min.

Gaut, Berys. "The Paradox of Horror." *Arguing About Art*. Eds. Alex Neil and Aaron Ridley. New York: Routledge. 2nd ed. 2002. 295-306.

Hoffner, Cynthia, and J. Cantor. "Factors Affecting Children's Enjoyment of a Frightening Film Sequence." *Communication Monographs*. 58 (1991): 41–62.

"Horror Story." *Compton's Encyclopedia*. 2nd ed. 1994.

Kreibig, Sylvia. "Cardiovascular, Electrodermal, and Respiratory Response Patterns to Fear- and Sadness-Inducing Films." *Psychophysiology*. 44(5): 787–806.

Pressley, Gretchen. "A Fascination With Fear." *The Columbia Missourian* 30 Oct. 2007. 1 Nov. 2007. <www.columbiamissourian.com/stories/2007/10/30/fascination-fear/>.

Andrade, Eduardo, and Joel Cohen. "On the Consumption of Negative Feelings." *Journal of Consumer Research* 34 (2007): 283–300.

Saw. DVD. Prod. Mark Burg, Daniel Jason Heffner, and Richard H. Prince. Dir. James Wan. Lionsgate. 100 min.

The Omen. DVD. Prod. John Moore, Jeffrey Stott, and Glenn Williamson. Dir. John Moore. 20th Century Fox, 2006. 110 min.

Wilson, Karina. "The Roots of the Genre." *Horror Film History*. 2005. 6 Nov 2007. <http://www.horrorfilmhistory.com/decades/early.html>.

Zillman, Dolf. "Arousal Processes and Media Effects." *Encyclopedia of Communication and Information*. MacMillan Reference USA. 1 Nov 2007. <http://www.bookrags.com/research/arousal-processes-and-media-effects-eci-01/>.

Inquiry
Sample Essay 2

WRTG 1150
Instructor: Nona Olivia

> The increase in cosmetic surgery is currently a subject of much debate. Olivia's essay goes beyond summarizing this trend to help us understand the ongoing and contradictory developments within feminism. By relating Makeover Feminism to significant questions about various feminist groups' changing perceptions of what it means to be liberated, Olivia gives the topic of cosmetic surgery a much-needed "facelift."

Makeover Feminism

OLIVIA KAHLO

Most viewers of commercial television or consumers of popular magazines have seen striking images of women whose appearance has been dramatically altered. Many of these "made-over" women changed their body image through diet and exercise regimes, skillfully applied makeup, or elective cosmetic surgery. Possessed of higher education, prestigious careers, and families, these successful women often report that they felt some aspect of their appearance prevented them from reaching their goals. Responding to criticism from feminists, they defend the choice to enhance their appearance as a tactical effort to win power in normative society. Drawing on popular media interpretations of third-wave feminism, women compelled to politicize a personal decision to "improve" their image have wrapped this act in ideological jargon.

"Makeover Feminism" is a cheeky new slogan meant to express the idea that conformity to cultural norms of physical beauty achieved through artificial and sometimes extreme means asserts female power. These women deny submission to patriarchal fantasies of the feminine ideal, claiming agency in the choice to alter their faces and/or bodies. Significant numbers of females submit to costly, dangerous, deforming, and potentially lethal procedures in an effort to claim power through beauty. This trend is visible in the annals of medical journal statistics that demonstrate an increase in the number of elective surgeries undergone by women in the last ten years (see Figure 1).

Year	Total Annual Procedures
1992	1,515,222.00
1996	1,937,877.00
2000	13,585,134.00
2001	13,254,795.00
2002	12,824,683.00
Total Number of Procedures	43,117,711.00

Figure 1

National Plastic Surgery Statistics

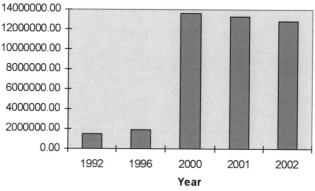

Figure 2

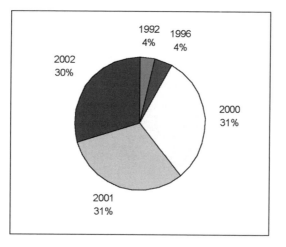

Figure 3
(Data courtesy of American Society of Plastic Surgeons)

These statistics (figures 2 and 3) indicate an overall increase in elective cosmetic procedures over the past decade. Further inquiry into this data source revealed the following: Women comprise 85% of cosmetic patients included in this database. Women 19–34 undergo a greater number of breast augmentation and Otoplasty (ear) surgeries, but women 35–50 account for 45% of female surgery patients (based on average numerical data from the American Society of Plastic Surgeons website from 1992–2002). The number one elective nonsurgical procedure is Botox injection, at an average cost of $400.00–450.00 per treatment, used to paralyze muscle and superficial fascia in order to prevent wrinkling from facial expression. The number one surgical procedure is cosmetic rhinoplasty, more commonly known as a "nose job," at an average fee of $3,500.00.

This data supports popular knowledge that cosmetics and cosmetic surgery is a multi-billion dollar industry, growing rich off the anxiety of Americans, especially women, who fear and dread aging, weight gain, or nonconformity to normative standards of appearance.

Research has shown that attractive people are hired and promoted more frequently, and also earn more income. Attractive women are perceived as friendlier and more competent than their non-attractive peers (Franzoi 374). Women, valued culturally for their sexual and reproductive role in the lives of men, uniquely suffer this association of virtue with beauty. Feminism traditionally attempts to deconstruct these cultural attributions by questioning the enshrinement of idealized feminine imagery in art, literature, theology, and law (for instance, iconic images of the Blessed Virgin Mary, or popular images perfect mothers such as Donna Read or June Cleaver). Feminists argue that women must be taken seriously as human beings that contribute to the community and the larger culture. Women should not to be valued solely as objects of male sexual gratification, or the surrogate means through which he may own his progeny. If women conform to the pressure to be beautiful, thin, and glamorous *just so they can have equal opportunities*, they capitulate to an oppressive patriarchal paradigm. Supporters of Makeover Feminism argue that positioning beauty and feminine sex appeal within dominant power structures—coupled with the skills, credentials, and authority to support those positions—undermines stereotypes of sexually attractive women as stupid and/or incapable. Although women obtain cultural power through beauty, and have every right to do so, it is nonetheless a contradiction in terms to call such tactics feminist. Makeover Feminism fails to construct political meaning or power for women, either psycho-socially or semantically.

The core ideologies of feminism are stood on their heads by apologists for the multi-billion dollar cosmetic industry, at the expense of a rich and valid feminist intellectual canon. I do not believe that women who choose cosmetic procedures make themselves enemies of feminism. The personal ethics of choosing to alter one's appearance is not at issue, but whether adaptation to an oppressive system in an attempt to gain power can be considered subversive. Beauty serves the individual in negotiating subtle (or not so subtle) dynamics of attraction and preference in the social competition for resources. However, this fails as a collective tool for political and socioeconomic revision of women's status. Women who gain power through cosmetically or surgically enhanced beauty do not create a stable base of power for all women. Further, by referring to their alterations as feminist actions, Makeover Feminists move the discourse of female meaning and power back into the realm of woman-as-object. This clearly violates the intention and agenda of traditional, socially-engaged feminism.

The construction of self-as-other has been the locus of feminist critique since at least the late 1700s when a Frenchwoman named Olympe de Gouges wrote and distributed a pamphlet entitled *Le Droits de la Femme* (The Rights of Woman). For her efforts, Olympe de Gouge was assassinated by guillotine (Donovan 1). In 1792 Mary Wollstonecraft published *A Vindication of the Rights of Women*, a response to Enlightenment-era discourse on the inalienable rights of men. Wollstonecraft recognized that women were confined to a position of objectification: "Strength of body and mind are sacrificed to libertine notions of beauty, to the desire of establishing themselves—the only way women can in the world—by marriage" (qtd. in Donovan 8). Although Wollstonecraft introduces the tension between woman's experience of herself as subject vs. object, the main thrust of her work centered on garnering civil rights for women. This original emphasis in feminism shaped first-wave feminist theory. Feminism's second wave penetrates social and political layers to explore psychological, religious, and philosophical understanding of misogyny. In 1949 Simone de Beauvoir wrote, "The situation of woman is that she—a free and autonomous being like all human creatures—nevertheless finds herself in a world where men compel her to assume the status of the Other" (qtd. in Donovan 117). It is not necessary to situate this argument within existentialism to understand the self-alienation implied by de Beauvoir's statement. A woman inhabiting an identity of Otherness lives from a displaced center; her actions and choices reflect the desires and preferences of the subject through whom she exists as other. Feminism, simply understood, seeks to redress this disassociation by establishing woman as subject.

The term Makeover Feminism may serve heuristically to summon concepts of individuality, choice, and embodiment. A woman undergoing surgeries, diets, hair coloring, and wardrobe transformations may be acting autonomously to recreate her image. However, the normative beauty standards against which she measures her image are probably not her own. It is always the patriarchal eye she is seeking to please, and through which she hopes to establish power. One doesn't hear, for instance, of a woman going under the knife to acquire a second chin in order to appear older, wiser, matriarchal, and therefore powerful. Claiming agency in her self-presentation, a woman conforming to normative standards of thinness and youthful appearance reinforces gendered subjugation to such standards. The truth behind the bravura of choice and agency in these women's arguments may be a bit more constrained. In fact, women who have been valued for their appearance and submissiveness all their lives may find it difficult to establish power through other means. One experiences great anxiety when moving from a familiar territory of power into new terrain. For women accustomed to the male gaze of approval, letting go of favored status as a pretty woman summons childhood fears of abandonment, and adult dread of the emptiness of death. For, if a self exists only as other, that self ceases to be if no longer "beheld."

Although feminist discourse on embodiment has become increasingly bizarre,[1] its original meaning centered on the immanent spiritual value of particularly female flesh. Feminists rewrote the female body as source of origin, nurturance, comfort, and the rooted center from which one lives a life of conscious negotiation with the world. Makeover Feminists position the self as object, and locate a woman's power in the act of being chosen. This brings us full circle in the argument for women's status as fully human beings that exist in, of, and for themselves primarily—as do men—not merely as relational creatures.

I would like to discuss briefly some theories and misunderstandings of third-wave feminism. In the 1980s authors such as Camille Paglia and Naomi Wolf emerged into the mainstream with new critiques of feminism that were accepted popularly as third-wave theory. In fact, these writers offered poor interpretations of second-wave feminist theory, reducing a complex evolution of feminist query to a single point—what they referred to as "victim feminism." Popular media, historically hostile to feminism, embraced these dissident voices, granting their arguments

[1] Feminist discourse on embodiment now includes arguments for and against cyborgs as representations of feminine consciousness, arguments for self-mutilation as gender performatives, Bordeau's defense of eating disorders as statement, and the ongoing discourse of appearance treated in this paper.

an authority not recognized in feminist academia. More respectably, the late 1970s and 1980s did bring some important criticism of feminism as a movement overly concerned with the issues facing white, educated, middle- and upper-class women. To quote feminist scholar Amanda Lotz, "During the 1970's and 1980's many women recognized that existing feminist theory was not sufficiently complex to understand or explain how oppression can be experienced differently within the broad category described as 'women'" (Lotz 4). The theories of women of color feminists and third-world feminists predate and better define academic third-wave feminism (Lotz 4) than do antagonists such as Paglia.

Regardless, popular theories of third-wave feminism persist, and include such new culture "power imagery" as Madonna, Buffy the Vampire Slayer, Kim Possible, the Spice Girls, Power Rangers, Britney Spears, Lara Croft, and Courtney Love.[2] Although these "power images" construct positive role models for girls and women, they reinforce normative feminine aesthetic standards. A woman's attainment of peak artistic, athletic, or intellectual mastery is seldom celebrated or rewarded in popular media unless paired with a pleasing face and body. Although each of these female icons perform skillfully and exhibit physical prowess rivaling any man, her intimidation factor is held in check by acquiescence to social norms of feminine hygiene and appearance. A beautiful, slender woman who "kicks ass" may find media approval, but an unshaven woman lawyer who makes partner before her male colleagues is a "granola dyke." The real message to women, I believe, is that powerful women are embraced *only* if they are thin, sexy, young, and beautiful.

Certainly, media figures exist who embody female agency and cultural power without conforming to ideals of feminine beauty. Former Secretary of State Madeline Albright, former Attorney General Janet Reno, and primatologist Jane Goodall inhabit public space as autonomous women seated in their own authority. Although these women have won cultural power, they are frequently criticized or humorously belittled for their appearance. In spite of this, I am not convinced that these women would have carved a deeper niche into the patriarchal belt by appearing younger, thinner or more buxom, or more obviously concerned with their sexual image. In fact, many beautiful, intelligent, capable women suggest that female attractiveness can be a hindrance as well as an asset. Some attractive women experience prejudice from teachers, colleagues, and employers who believe that a pretty woman cannot be bright. Other beautiful, successful women have endured accusations of having "slept their way" to positions of power. This no-win situation for women is what anthropologist Gregory Bateson termed

---

[2] Interestingly, I stumbled across the phrase "makeover feminism" in an online article analyzing Courtney Love's physical transformation.

a double bind (qtd. in Laing 113). The problem then shifts from media manipulation of imagery to the psychosexual arena of gender politics, and this is where feminists must situate their struggle.

Makeover Feminists will argue that they situate the problem appropriately by asserting their right to be beautiful, sexual, self-determining in their aesthetic choices, *and* use these tools to wrest power from the brokers. I agree that women must reclaim their sexual nature, and even see the possible realm of embodied power as "other" if played with consciously. However, a social movement for liberation must include all expressions of a true self: instincts, drives, needs, and desires for things basic to survival, for relationship, and for transcendence. One cannot live a fully authentic life as object/other without recourse to varied states of empowered being. It is impossible to build a free society if the psyche is split and enslaved to shadow projections.

As previously asserted, feminism is basically a shift from woman as eternal Other—always defined from outside—to woman as Self. Makeover Feminism, despite its sincere discourse within the tradition, cannot accomplish the goal of female liberation.

Works Cited

American Society of Plastic Surgeons. <http://www.plasticsurgery.org>.

Donovan, Josephine. *Feminist Theory: The Intellectual Traditions of American Feminism*. New York: Continuum, 1992.

Franzoi, *Stephen L. Social Psychology*. 3rd ed. New York: McGraw-Hill, 2003.

Laing, R.D. *The Politics of Experience*. New York: Ballantine, 1973.

Lotz, Amanda D. "Communicating Third-Wave Feminism and New Social Movements: Challenges for the Next Century of Feminist Endeavor." *Women and Language* 26.1 (2003): 2–9.

Inquiry
Sample Essay 3 (Research Proposal and Literature Review)

WRTG 1150
Instructor: Judith Lavinsky

> This assignment asked students to review the significant information they had gathered through research relating to their chosen topics. In the literature review, Brad focuses his discussion of his sources on ideas and information specifically relevant for his topic—an exploration of why students leave college. By discussing how the information, ideas, and arguments in the various sources support, contradict, and converse with each other, Brad supports his research proposal and lays the foundation for using this research in pursuit of his own inquiry.

Theories on Student Attrition

BRAD HALD

Research Proposal

As a former college dropout, "student attrition" is a subject that carries great interest for me. I am curious to discover whether my motive for leaving has been shared by others, and if not, I would like to learn alternate reasons. My hope is that I will find a significant section of college dropouts who have made that choice for positive reasons, rather than simply failing out. Because higher education has proved its worth in all aspects of society, this field of study is undoubtedly one of great importance. College-educated men and women earn higher salaries, make better decisions in life, and produce children who share their own value of knowledge. I would guess that relationships exist between dropout and financial situation, grades, etc., and I also hope to discover a relationship between dropout rates and students' ability or inability to immerse themselves in the new college community and lifestyle.

We face a daunting set of decisions in college life, and we doubtless all respond differently to these pressures. In preliminary research, I have found a number of studies and various theories on this very topic. From these studies I propose an in-depth research project with the purpose of expounding the relevant attrition theories and models. Several accredited experts in the field of student attrition have published voluminous works, such as Vincent Tinto and John Bean. Perhaps the best resource for further primary source material comes from the bibliographies of these authors, which I will utilize to find a sample of the actual studies on which these theories are based. The various psychological, sociological, and education (specifically, ERIC) databases contained within the university library system may also provide ample material.

Literature Review

Since the early seventies, theorists have pondered the causes of college dropout. Generally referred to as "student attrition," this problem has spurred numerous causal theories and theoretical models. Vincent Tinto led the research with his revolutionary 1973 study, which he later revised in 1987 amid criticism. Some of those early critics include Bean, Astin, Terenzini, and Pascarella; it is on the work of these scholars (including Tinto) that all modern research in the student attrition field is based. In this paper, I will first review in brief some of the extensive research from Tinto to the present, including the basic criticisms therein, and then go on to explain the steps some colleges are currently taking to address this increasingly important issue.

Little or no research was conducted on student attrition prior to Tinto, and every piece of research I found contained several references to him and his work. Ishitani and DesJardins claim that the majority of research on the subject has been based on Tinto's model (7), as does Metz in his research review (4). Metz, however, goes on to assert that Tinto's main source was a certain *Rites of Passage*, by Arnold van Gennep. Focusing on the anthropological perspective of human "rites of passage," van Gennep's study elucidates the basic human nature behind much of the college experience. Tinto primarily utilizes the chapter entitled "Initiation Rites" in his model, a chapter in which van Gennep claims "that physiological puberty and 'social puberty' are essentially different" (65). Tinto sees the transition from high school to college as a form of this "social puberty." He further argues that the maturation process is "marked by three distinct phases or stages, each with its own specialized ceremonies and rituals," and "[e]ach serv[ing] to move individuals from youthful participation to full adult membership in society" (Tinto 92). College, according to van Gennep and Tinto, therefore, is simply part of this sociological maturation process.

Tinto's original theory involved five specific factors that contributed to student retention. They were: 1) a student's pre-entry attributes (prior schooling and family background); 2) goals and commitment (the student's individual aspirations in the institution); 3) experience at the institution (academics and faculty and peer interactions); 4) external commitments while at the institution; and 5) integration both academically and socially (Metz 4). In the second edition of his book, Tinto argues against models of attrition that "see student departure as reflecting some shortcoming and/or weakness in the individual," further reinforcing the fifth aspect of his attrition model: the subjective category of integration (Tinto 85). In essence, Tinto is arguing that a student may be passing classes with flying colors and still decide to drop out for reasons unrelated to "shortcoming and/or weakness," and that the act of dropping out should not necessarily carry a negative connotation.

This first theory has, of course, since been criticized and manipulated to fit later theories in the collective effort to create a single unifying attrition model. In his "involvement theory," Astin "suggested certain variables influence student persistence, notably various forms of financial aid," and that "students learn by becoming involved" in college-sponsored activities (Metz 5). Although Tinto certainly includes the latter in his theory, he clearly ignores the former argument of Astin.

John Bean further "expanded on the previous work of Tinto and Astin by integrating academic variables, student intent, goals, expectations, and external and internal environmental factors into a revised model of persistence" (Metz 8). Bean criticizes Tinto for not citing "similarities between leaving the world of work and leaving college," suggesting reasons might be similar between the two (Metz 8). Bean's attrition model includes another set of five facets; they are: 1) routinization—the idea that student life becomes routine; 2) instrumental communication—how well an institution distributes information about student life; 3) participation in classroom decisions; 4) integration; and 5) distributive justice—whether rewards are consistent with effort expended (Ishitani and DesJardins 6–7). Both Metz and Ishitani and DesJardins agree that "Most researchers have used one of these models [Tinto or Bean] to explain student departure" (Ishitani and DesJardins 7).

Later scholars have continued to criticize other aspects of Tinto's theory. Tierney argues against Tinto's reliance on a traditional age for college students, which ignores a large number of older, returning students (Metz 9). Others have argued against the theory for its ignorance of the two-year college, and for its failure to take into account the differing circumstances of minority students.

Ishitani and DesJardins bring a more compelling criticism in their five-year study of student attrition. While Tinto's model assumes the various forces on the student remain constant throughout the college experience, Ishitani and DesJardins argue that these forces vary from year to year. Dividing the student group into different subsets based on family income, SAT scores, gender, race, and, subsequently, first-year GPA, their study yielded interesting results (11). While most of the results were expected (e.g., higher income, GPA, and SAT scores equated with higher likelihood of retention), a few varied from year to year. For example, "the provision of financial aid in year three substantially reduces dropout behavior relative to the non-receipt of aid" (22). Another unexpected finding was that first-year students who met with faculty out of the classroom were 25% more likely to drop out than those who did not interact with faculty (20). Clearly, then, the significance of this experiment is that it proves Tinto's theory is fundamentally flawed, as dropout variables change from year to year.

All of this is to say that students and scholars still await a single, unifying theory of attrition. In the absence of such a theory, colleges are now attempting new strategies by adding incentives for student retention. Southwest Texas State University has implemented "learning communities" designed to engage freshman in school activities and thus help them with the integration process that, as pointed out by Tinto and Bean, among others, is so critical to retention (Reisberg 2). Other institutions have introduced a tuition credit for students who stay enrolled for a certain amount of time (Reisberg 3). Minnesota State University, Mankato created cluster courses designed to help students bond with one another during the first year away from home, and the university had seen its retention rate increase 10% in its first five years (Reisberg 4). Colleges such as these utilize the various attrition theories in an effort to identify those students who are at risk of dropping out, and these students are the reason that past and future research remains important.

While student attrition research has certainly come a long way since Vincent Tinto, in many ways it has stayed the same. His theories still form the foundation for all modern scholarship. The various criticisms of subsequent scholars have only served to make this foundation stronger and further evolved. Colleges today have more resources for improving student retention than ever before; with continued research and study, they will continue to ensure the spread of higher education.

Bibliography

Gennep, Arnold van. *The Rites of Passage*. Chicago: U of Chicago P, 1960.

Ishitani, Terry T. and Stephen L. DesJardins. "A Longitudinal Investigation of Dropout from College in the United States. AIR 2002 Forum Paper." ERIC ED473067. 4 June 2002: 1–34.

Metz, George W. "Challenges and Changes to Tinto's Persistence Theory." ERIC ED471529. October 2002: 1–28.

Reisberg, Leo. "Colleges Struggle to Keep Would-Be Dropouts Enrolled." *Chronicle of Higher Education* 8 October 1999: 54–57.

Tinto, Vincent. *Leaving College: Rethinking the Causes and Cures of Student Attrition*. 2nd Ed. Chicago: U of Chicago P, 1993.

Argument
Sample Essay 1

WRTG 1250
Instructor: Christine MacDonald

> The latest Britney report, the celebrity baby update — is this news? In this essay, Marcy argues that mainstream news media need to rethink their mission. While she acknowledges that celebrity news has some value (a strategy that demonstrates her understanding of the opposition), she counters that the bulk of celebrity news should be contained to specialized media outlets, rather than overrunning mainstream news media.

America's Obsession with Celebrities and Celebrity News: When Is It Too Much?

MARCY FRANKLIN

One typical morning, I flipped the channel to CNN to catch up on my current events. I saw uninterrupted coverage with serious anchors and reporters giving the grave news that someone had died. My first instinct told me that it was someone who carried a lot of importance in society; perhaps it was a politician, a humanitarian, or a celebrity. Sure enough, in due time I learned that it was Anna Nicole Smith. She was just a girl famous for being famous, a Playboy bunny who frequently graced the cover of tabloids for her less-than-flattering antics. I then checked my local newspapers' websites and saw more disturbing news: Britney Spears had shaved her head. And from there it was a downhill slide. I had to learn more about how Anna died, why Britney shaved her head, why an acclaimed NASA astronaut wore diapers to drive 900 miles to harass her competition for another astronaut's heart... But why did I even care? Why was it so important for me to know who Anna's baby's father was, when I certainly wasn't a fan of hers before her death? It didn't seem all that important to me, and yet I couldn't stop reading these stories.

It is a question that must be asked in our celebrity culture: Why do we care? What possesses us to keep up on our celebrity news? It comes as no surprise that our society is obsessed, mesmerized with fame. We want to be near it, we want to have it as our own. Jake Halpern, the author of *Fame Junkies: The Hidden Truths Behind America's Addiction*, noted a survey given to 635 middle school students in Rochester, New York. One question asked was with whom they would most like to have dinner. The clear winner, with 17.4 percent, was awarded to Jennifer

Lopez. Jesus Christ came in second with 16.8 percent, and Paris Hilton and 50 Cent tied for third with 15.8 percent (Halpern xvi). Additionally, when students were asked to rank which job they would most like to have in the future, the clear winner was the job of a celebrity personal assistant, sweeping the contest with 43.4 percent (Halpern xvi). The children of our nation, according to these results, are more interested in fame and celebrities rather than the scholars and leaders of our time. What is even more disturbing is that children are not even aspiring to necessarily *be* famous—they want to *assist* celebrities. They are more willing to be a servant to fame rather than do something noteworthy with their own lives.

Appalling as the results may be, who are we to blame? The finger points in the direction of the media. During the Anna Nicole Smith saga, the mainstream media outlets neglected to inform the public that Al Qaeda had been building operatives in Pakistan that were steadily growing (Herbert, para. 7). Rather, the public was inundated with the news from the Anna Nicole melodrama. And the entertainment business is multiplying daily, while the news industry is on the decline. The talent competition *American Idol* brings in more viewers than the nightly news on NBC, ABC, and CBS combined (Halpern xv). Is our obsession with fame blinding us to the important events and issues of our time, or do we simply ignore them? More importantly, is the media emphasizing celebrity news over hard news, and why?

As a journalism major, I have been faithfully taught that the purpose of journalism is to inform citizens so that we can be a free and self-governing society. It seems so simple and clear-cut to us in theory, but it is harder to act on those purposes. When I see the overwhelming amount of celebrity coverage in the media, it makes me question whether the media is fulfilling its journalistic purpose. It is the role, the responsibility, of the media to give us the information that citizens need to be self-governing. It is essential that the media give us the news that helps our democracy to be self-governing; it is clear that celebrity news is hindering our society's ability to be independent and free.

Many will argue that there is nothing inherently wrong with celebrity news, especially in the form of tabloid journalism. Henrik Ornebring, of the University of Leicester in the UK, and Anna Maria Jonnson, of the Goteburg University and Sodertom University College of Sweden, argue that tabloid journalism is not simply another synonym for "bad" journalism. The authors stress that the mainstream media creates a need for an alternative media to present different issues. The problem, these professors argue, is that these alternative media outlets, especially tabloids, are labeled as deterrents to serving the public interest. The authors write,

Lay (and sometimes academic) criticism of journalism continues to be based around simple binary oppositions, where emotional is bad and rational-intellectual is good, sensation is contrasted with contextualisation and tabloid journalism is charged with meeting complexity with dumbing down. But emotionalism, sensation and simplification are not *necessarily* opposed to serving the public good. (Ornebring and Jonsson 284)

As the authors mention later, tabloid journalism throughout history has attracted a new public by discussing issues that have been ignored in the mainstream media, therefore better serving the public interest (Ornebring and Jonsson 287). Celebrity news has a similar effect on the public; celebrity gossip media outlets like the E! Channel or *People* magazine bring in audiences looking for celebrity gossip that is not found in mainstream media.

Furthermore, some argue that interest in celebrities, or as psychology professionals define it, "celebrity worship," is not necessarily a bad thing. According to a psychological study, low levels of celebrity worship correlate with high levels of extraversion in people. Psychology researchers John Maltby, Liza Day, Lynn E. McCutcheon, Raphael Gillett, James Houran, and Diane D. Ashe write, "Celebrity worshippers who do so for entertainment-social reasons are extraverted, seek information and support, and are able to display emotions" (423). These characteristics defend the purpose behind celebrity news. Bonnie Fuller, the chief editorial director for American Media Inc., the tabloid conglomerate that publishes the *Star*, the *National Enquirer*, and the *Globe*, said,

What's going on is that we all have fewer people in common. When you're in high school, or at a small college, you know everybody's business and you can follow their romantic goings-on and discuss them with your friends. But when you grow up and you're out in the work world, you don't have that. So celebrities give us a whole world of people in common—people to gossip about at work over the water cooler or at a dinner party. (Halpern 147)

Celebrity news then serves to bring people together socially and give people an escape from mainstream media. Fuller's argument then seems to justify the validity of celebrity news. However, it should be noted that Fuller's career depends on the validity of celebrity news.

This is not a paper criticizing people's desire to learn about celebrities. However, I believe that the argument that celebrity news is valid within the mainstream media contains loopholes too big to ignore. I will concede that celebrity news is not a bad thing when it is contained to alternative media outlets like the E! channel or *People* magazine. These media outlets are no different than any other specialized media—for example, a sports channel or a sports magazine. This is because they cater to the audience's interests, and indeed, there is a very large audience that is interested in celebrities. But when celebrity news crowds out other news on mainstream media outlets, then it becomes a problem. It has changed what news agencies are pursuing as news. Sue Cross, a vice president of the Associated Press, reported that the news wire service now gets requests from as far away as Indonesia and Germany to report on celebrity stories (Merina, para. 32). Additionally, a study done by Thomas Patterson of Harvard University found that, from 1987 to 2001, "soft" news stories, which includes celebrity news, have increased from 35 percent of stories to 50 percent of stories (Valencia, para. 6). Celebrity news is taking up valuable space, time, and resources that could be dedicated to pursuing stories that make a difference in society.

The Anna Nicole saga may be the most recent prime example. The amount of airtime, page space, and resources dedicated to following the drama was overwhelming in comparison to the coverage of other news stories. Nick Madigan of the *Baltimore Sun* reported in his editorial that according to the Project for Excellence in Journalism, the Smith story was the number-one story on cable television for a week, and that it took up half the news airtime in the first two days after her death (Madigan, para. 21). In addition, the major mainstream media outlets spent more time dedicated to Smith's story than a developing story about the haphazard conditions and substandard care for wounded soldiers at the Walter Reed Army Medical Center. One website that tracks media coverage, TheLeftCoaster.com, tracked the number of references to the Smith story and the Walter Reed story on news networks. On March 2, Fox News had 10 references to the Walter Reed story, compared to an astounding 121 references to Anna Nicole Smith. The other mainstream media outlets did not fare much better than Fox News; MSNBC had 84 references to Walter Reed compared to 96 to Anna Nicole. CNN, which appeared to be more serious in its news-gathering, had 53 mentions of Walter Reed compared to 40 references to Anna Nicole (Madigan, para. 22). These reports are dismal and shocking. Perhaps it is no wonder that we as Americans are claimed to be uninformed about important issues of our time. When the media should be providing news about an issue that affects numerous people, citizens are instead learning more about a Playboy bunny whose fame was inherent only after death.

This is not to say that Anna Nicole's death has no worth as a breaking news story. But a mention on mainstream media outlets would certainly have sufficed; there are numerous celebrity news outlets to cover her death. Continuing with the arguments of Ornebring and Jonsson, if the mainstream media have created alternative media outlets, then celebrity news should be kept to those outlets. If people wish to learn about their favorite celebrities, then by all means, they have an abundant number of outlets to choose from. Celebrity news has no place in the mainstream media; there are more than plenty of alternative media outlets to cover celebrities.

However, many argue that celebrity news is needed for the news industry to survive. Another argument in favor of celebrity journalism in mainstream media is that the media industry needs celebrity news to boost its ratings or circulation numbers. Undoubtedly, mediums such as newspapers are losing readers rapidly. But while circulation numbers and ratings are decreasing, the "infotainment" industry is booming. *People*, *Us Weekly*, *InStyle* and *Entertainment Weekly* magazines saw an increase of 18.7 percent in circulation; news magazines like *Time*, *Newsweek*, *The New Yorker* and *The Atlantic* saw an increase of 2 percent (Halpern xv). As a result, mainstream media outlets are hopping on the tabloid bandwagon. Jay T. Harris, a former editor of a big city tabloid and the Wallis Annenberg Chair in the Annenberg School of Communication at USC, acknowledged the advantages sensational celebrity news has for journalists. In his opinion, it is undeniable that celebrity coverage sells. In an article for the conference "Reporting on Celebrities: The Ethics of News Coverage," he wrote,

> I guess journalists could argue that celebrity coverage is smart business. Further, I will stipulate that, by extension, competitive pressures provide a plausible justification for celebrity coverage — if I don't do it my competitor will and that will be to my disadvantage. (Harris, para. 6)

If the media believe that celebrity news can rescue them from dismal numbers, then they will certainly keep giving their audiences more sensational news. There is, however, a problem with this rationale. Because celebrity news is able to raise circulation and ratings numbers, this leads to the belief that people must want more coverage of celebrities rather than real news stories.

Although the media seem to believe that their audiences want more celebrity news, it is not necessarily true. The world's largest news agency, the Associated Press, decided in February of 2007 to suspend temporarily its coverage of the famous heiress, Paris Hilton. Editors wanted to see the results if they didn't publish any stories about Hilton (Madigan, para. 3). At about the same time, on February 9, 2007 Brian Williams, the anchor of NBC's Nightly News, posted on his web log, the Daily Nightly, "Viewer warning: There will be no mention of Britney Spears' baldness or rehab in tonight's broadcast, nor will there be any mention of Anna Nicole's 'body possession' hearing" (Deggans, para. 2). He said later,

> I wrote it on a whim...I realized I was watching three cable news networks do-
> ing some combination (of stories) on a bald singer leaving rehab for a second
> time and a dead former Playmate whose body is being argued over. I've got a
> world to cover...(and) if I thought for a moment that Nightly News was some-
> how depriving a yearning nation of these twin tragedies, I would rethink that
> decision. (Deggans, para. 4)

Now, was there uproar over Williams's decision to not give time to
Britney and Paris? Were news agencies clamoring for more Paris stories from the Associated Press? Not quite. The Associated Press, to its
surprise, found that no one requested any Paris stories during its suspen-
sion, athough, in all fairness, the agency did note that nothing out of the
ordinary happened to Hilton: "No [media outlet] felt a newsworthy event
had been ignored" (Madigan, para. 6). Rem Reider, an editor for the
American Journalism Review, agreed that the AP's experiment exposed
something about the American public. He was quoted as saying; "I don't
think the world would be diminished if there were a Paris Hilton black-
out—with all respect to Paris Hilton" (Madigan, para. 1). Brian Williams
found support for his decision from his viewers. Comments on his blog
were actually in support of his decision. Wrote Matthew Cowan Mechan-
icsburg of Pennsylvania, "Your judgment is excellent. I was so glad to see
some news last night. I was afraid I'd see nothing but Anna Nicole" (Williams 2007). Williams even responded to those who opposed his decision
to not give Smith any coverage. He said that if people disagreed with his
editorial decision, they could get that news from a number of other news
sources. He wrote on his blog,

> It's not as if there aren't other news outlets for those viewers dissatisfied with our
> treatment of the story and the end of a tragic life. People watch our broadcast
> presumably because they trust our reporting and our people, and because they
> agree with our editorial take on the day more often than not. The great thing
> about this era of media choice is that all those who find our broadcast lacking
> in any way are free to go to any number of Web sites where they can find video
> showing a cat flushing a toilet, or the explosive properties of Diet Coke and
> Mentos when mixed together. (Williams, para. 2)

However, Williams did receive some criticism for not covering Smith.
Wrote Eric Deggans in an editorial in the *St. Petersburg Times*, a respect-
ed journalist like Williams could have provided an insightful look into
Smith's story rather than the mindless coverage on every cable channel
(Deggans, para. 7). But Williams recognized that people do not want as
much celebrity news as the media believe.

In fact, the study by Patterson found that audiences actually *preferred* issue stories rather than soft news stories, celebrity news included. The study, which looked at over 5,000 stories from the LexisNexis database of two television networks, three prominent newspapers, and 26 local dailies, found that the foundation of news audiences are those who read hard news stories (Valencia, para. 12). People look to the mainstream media outlets to get the news, not to be informed of the latest celebrity happenings.

Furthermore, some argue that using the "infotainment" strategy actually hurts rather than helps news organizations in the end. Media scholars Bill Kovach and Tom Rosenstiel argue that when news turns into entertainment, news organizations must compete with media other than their own, a competition that they cannot win (154). "Infotainment" also creates audiences that are not reliable in terms of ratings and circulation numbers. Kovach and Rosenstiel write,

> The strategy of infotainment, though it may attract an audience in the short run and may be cheap to produce, will build a shallow audience because it is built on form, not substance. Such an audience will switch to the next "most exciting" thing because it was built on the spongy ground of excitement in the first place. (155)

The media's argument that validates celebrity news's worth in the mainstream media is therefore faulty. Celebrity news doesn't just hurt the audiences, but it hurts news organizations as well. In a time when the news industry is struggling to survive, news organizations should be wary of the dangers that celebrity news has.

Therefore, celebrity news is a viable threat to both our media and our democracy. According to Kovach and Rosenstiel, the primary purpose of journalism is "to provide citizens with the information they need to be free and self-governing" (17). The media have a responsibility to citizens to inform the public, or democracy suffers. Jay T. Harris, a former editor of a big-city tabloid and the Wallis Annenberg Chair in the Annenberg School of Communication at USC, sees the possible damage that celebrity news has for the future of our society. He said,

> We [journalists] are the essential plumbing—we carry useful information, including information on changing values, priorities, and shared challenges. But we also carry (or maybe spread is the better word here) that which weakens, that which corrodes, that which debases. (Harris, para. 9)

Additionally, actor Ed Asner, at the "Reporting on Celebrities: The Ethics of News Coverage" conference, called out celebrity news for contributing to the "moral decay" of the country (Merina, para. 39). It's ironic that such harsh criticism of the journalism field comes from an actor, who is one of the many players in the crisis of celebrity news.

So then, what are the consequences of celebrity news? Why is it so damaging to our democracy? We can look to the theory of agenda-setting to explain the possible effects of too much celebrity news. According to the book *Questioning the Media: A Critical Introduction*, the news media have the power to define what is news and what is not. Therefore, whatever the news media give the most prominence to, we consider to be news and important. The definition reads, "News media power is based not so much on how the media interpret events to us as it is on the sheer fact that they can set our agenda of things to think about in the first place" (Downing et al., 478). To follow this theory, if mainstream media are emphasizing celebrity news over important news stories, then we are more likely to think about celebrities rather than the issues that are pertinent to our democracy. The consequences of this are huge. Suppose that all we cared about is Anna Nicole's baby or Britney's meltdown rather than the issues that make a difference in our lives. How can a democracy possibly survive on paparazzi photographs and celebrity hook-ups without the information it needs to be self-governing? It cannot. Famed journalist Edward R. Murrow put it wisely in 1958, to the Radio-Television News Directors Association Convention, "For surely we shall pay for using this most powerful instrument of communication [television] to insulate the citizenry from the hard and demanding realities which must be faced if we are to survive. I mean the word survive literally" (para. 5). Journalists cannot insulate citizens with celebrity gossip, for it will be detrimental to society.

In all of my research, I found that no one in the journalism field was eager to take sides on the issue. Although many were quick to gripe about the huge amount of celebrity news that appears in mainstream media, they also recognize that without it, news media would not survive. Although many see celebrity news as demeaning to their work, they also realize that many people want it. So then, what are mainstream media to do? Do they run by profits and market demands or by what they believe to be right? Do they give citizens more celebrity news or the news that they see as important? Who, then, decides what news is important and what news audiences need? These are questions with no easy answers. But it distresses me greatly to see that my work in the future, the field and career that I am committed to, may be diminished to following trails of the latest celebrity gossip. I certainly didn't become interested in the field of journalism because I wanted to follow rumors of Britney Spears's antics. I became passionate about journalism because I believed that the stories that I would write would make a difference in my democracy, in my society. Do stories about Britney Spears indeed help the citizens and make a difference? For entertainment purposes, maybe, but I would have to argue they do not inherently help citizens. But I will continue to believe, with perhaps a bit of blind optimism, that the purpose of journalism is not to simply give audiences fluff, information that they do not need. I will believe that the purpose of journalism still is, and always will be, to provide the citizens with information that our democracy needs to function. Therefore, I urge the entire mainstream media to retrace its steps back to the roots and principles of journalism. I challenge the industry to think outside the market demands, the world of ratings and circulation numbers, and to once again consider the audience and what it needs. As Kovach and Rosenstiel worded it so eloquently, journalism's first loyalty is to the citizens, and its first obligation is to provide those citizens with the information they need (13). Celebrity news in the mainstream media is hindering our news industry from fulfilling its journalistic duties, and in turn hurting the citizens of our democracy.

Works Cited

Deggans, Eric. "Anna Nicole and Britney? Yes, they are news." *St. Petersburg Times*. 27 Feb. 2007. LexisNexis. Boulder, CO. 14 Mar. 2007. <http://ucblibraries.colorado.edu>.

Downing, John, Ali Mohammadi, and Annabelle Sreberny-Mohammadi. *Questioning the Media: a Critical Introduction*. 2nd ed. Thousand Oaks, CA: Sage Publications, 1995.

Herbert, Bob. "From Anna to Britney to Zawahri." *The New York Times* 2007. LexisNexis. Boulder, CO. 26 Feb. 2007. <http://ucblibraries. colorado.edu>.

Halpern, Jake. *Fame Junkies: the Hidden Truths Behind America's Favorite Addiction*. New York: Houghton Mifflin Company, 2007.

Harris, Jay T. "Why Do We Care About Celebrities?" *Poynter Online*. 21 Jan. 2004. Poynter Institute. 21 Mar. 2007. <www.poynter.org>.

Kovach, Bill and Tom Rosenstiel. *The Elements of Journalism*. New York, NY: Three Rivers P, 2001. 187–207.

Madigan, Nick. "Media Say 'Enough Already.'" *The Baltimore Sun*. 11 Mar. 2007. LexisNexis. Boulder, CO. 14 Mar. 2007. <http://ucblibraries. colorado.edu>.

Maltby, John, Liza Day, Lynn E. McCutcheon, Raphael Gillett, James Houran, and Diane D. Ashe. "Personality and Coping: a Context for Examining Celebrity Worship and Mental Health." *British Journal of Psychology* 95 (2004): 411-428. Thomson Gale. Boulder, CO. 23 Feb. 2007. <http://ucblibraries.colorado.edu>.

Merina, Victor. "Celebrities in Journalism: the Ethics of News Coverage." *Poynter Online*. 22 Jan. 2004. Poynter Institute. 23 Feb. 2007 <www.poynter.org>.

Murrow, Edward R. "Keynote Speeches." *Radio-Television News Directors Association*. The Association of Electronic Journalists. 18 Apr. 2007 <www.rtnda.org>.

Ornebring, Henrik and Anna Maria Jonsson. "Tabloid Journalism and the Public Sphere: A Historical Perspective on Tabloid Journalism." *Journalism Studies* 5 (2004): 283-295. Academic Search Premier. Boulder, CO. 23 Feb. 2007. <http://ucblibraries.colorado.edu>

Valencia, Monica. "The Wet Stuff, the White Stuff and the Pooch: Sensationalism and Gossip in News." *Poynter Online*. 21 Aug. 2001. Poynter Institute. 14 Feb. 2007 <www.poynter.org>.

Williams, Brian. "About Last Night ..." MSNBC. 9 Feb. 2007. 21 Mar. 2007. <http://dailynightly.msnbc.com/2007/02/post_1.html#comments>.

Argument
Sample Essay 2

WRTG 1150
Instructor: Tobin von der Nuell

> In this essay, Danielle is responding to an assignment that invited her to present her position on a clearly established issue. In doing so, she uses various types of writing—summary, analysis, refutation, narrative, and inquiry—to make her point. By arguing her own position, Danielle joins the larger conversation about the usefulness (or uselessness) of the SAT.

The New SAT: Is It a Better Assessment of How a Student Will Perform in College?

DANIELLE KOFFLER

The night before the last SAT we would ever take, my friend and I met with our SAT tutor to have one final study session. We reviewed all that we had learned, we complained, and we even ate fish, because apparently that makes you think better. We both got the full recommended eight hours of sleep, and we wore yellow to help "stimulate" our brains. When we arrived at school at 7:30 a.m. on Saturday morning, we were surrounded by several hundred other anxious high school students cramming a few final vocabulary words. The general sentiment was one of nervousness and frustration, because we all knew that how we performed over the next three hours was going to be one of the deciding factors of where we would be next year. Colleges and universities may see the Scholastic Aptitude Test as an indicator of how well you will do in college, but the students taking it consider it to be a long, boring, and overwhelming test with the power to determine their futures. Students will do anything, no matter how superstitious or absurd, to score as high as possible on the test.

For the past sixty-three years, high school students have been plagued by the SAT. During that time, the test has become a critical aspect in the college admissions process, and students have come to see it as the crucial component of their applications. However, it has been argued that, instead of accurately predicting how students will perform once they are in college, the SAT simply determines whether or not they will get to spend the next four years at the top college on their list. For years now, there have been complaints that the SAT does not adequately test a student's capabilities in college and that it is biased in design, and the College Board is finally making necessary changes. Specifically, it has altered the verbal and math sections and added a writing section. However, further inquiry into these changes reveals that, while this new test is making positive steps towards becoming a more standardized test, it is still not an accurate assessment of how a student will do in college, and it remains biased against women and minorities.

Several changes have been made to the math and verbal sections. The math section now includes Algebra II instead of just geometry and Algebra I, and the quantitative comparisons have been deleted. The verbal section, soon to be called the Critical Reading Section, no longer has analogies in it, just more short reading passages. And finally, the new writing section will be composed of a written essay and multiple-choice questions on grammar and usage. With these alterations, the new test will now last an excruciatingly long three hours and forty-five minutes with 2400 points possible, as opposed to the old test, which lasted only three hours and had 1600 points possible (Henriques). Because of the addition of the writing section, the cost to take the SAT will also increase by a little over $10, making it a whopping $41. Each of these changes has an impact on the performance of high school students around the country on the dreaded SATs.

The adjustments made to the SAT should improve the test's ability to predict how a student will perform in college. Incorporating Algebra II level math should improve scores, because, unlike geometry, which is usually taken in early years of high school and thus forgotten by the time the student is ready to take the SAT, Algebra is taken in later years and is still fresh in students' minds. It is therefore more relevant to our "current curriculum and institutional practices" (Engelberg and Frank). The essay on the new SAT will also greatly increase a college's ability to determine how a student will do in college because essays reveal whether or not students can formulate their own ideas, a skill that is strongly emphasized in college curriculum. This skill is "essential to college success" and is much more important than being able to regurgitate information, since college requires more written essays than standardized tests in most areas of learning (Henriques). Furthermore, adding a writing section to the SAT will help "return writing to its rightful place in American education," since students will now have to focus on it more (Fitzsimmons).

The previous SAT not only tested material that was irrelevant to students' current studies, but it was also biased against women and minorities. It has been found that males are usually more successful on the math sections of the SAT, mostly due to the fact that females use their intuition and personal experiences instead of the more objective methods that males use (Clewell and Anderson). Because of this difference, females envision math as a "male activity," resulting in even lower math grades and scores (Clewell and Anderson). In 1989, it was ruled in federal court that the SATs did show a bias against females, thus making awards won through SAT scores unfair (Glaberson). Minorities also differ in their SAT scores, and the score gaps are even greater than those between genders (Clewell and Anderson). Minorities are at a disadvantage for the SAT, since they typically receive lesser quality educations, equipment, and resources ("New SAT").

Through my experiences in high school, I found that, while there may be exceptions, overall these claimed biases are true. I was one of the select few in my large group of girlfriends in high school who did better on the math section than on the verbal section. Furthermore, there was not a significant minority population at the prep school I attended because it was too expensive for most of the minority population living in the area to attend. So a large portion of the minorities were forced to attend the public schools that did not give nearly as much preparation as my school did for the SATs.

The new SAT has done little to help balance these old biases. The addition of a writing section and more advanced math will hurt minorities. Discrimination in the writing section could occur because the educators grading the writing section might be inclined to prefer more refined writing styles that are not as emphasized in the public schools that many minorities have to attend. In addition, more white students take higher-level math classes than minority students, so by making the math section harder, the test puts minorities at an even greater disadvantage. Some believe that these changes will actually increase the education gap between minority and white students, because teachers will teach to the test instead of teaching minorities "raw intellectual power" ("New SAT"). In other words, students will be taught how to answer SAT-style multiple-choice questions instead of really learning the more important skills that will be more useful to them in college. After all, it is of no benefit to achieve a high SAT score if all you know is how to answer multiple choice questions, because once enrolled in college you will be at a complete disadvantage.

Where females are concerned, the changes are likely to both help and harm performance. On the one hand, the writing section will likely improve females' scores since women typically are better at writing essays than answering multiple-choice questions, because of the fact that, as mentioned earlier, they use intuition and personal experience in testing situations, thus making an essay easier to answer than an objective multiple-choice question. But this advantage will be counteracted in the math section since it is now harder, which may consequently result in women performing worse.

Finally, not only will the new SAT reinforce pre-existing biases, but it also creates new ones. Now the test is biased against males, who are usually better at multiple choice, and also people who are incapable of writing good essays quickly, even though they do formulate good ideas and write great essays when given large blocks of time. In addition, the new writing section cannot be graded by Scantron, and therefore must be graded by humans, potentially introducing a whole new range of biases.

In a broader sense, the test is still not a strong assessment of how any student, no matter what race or gender, will do in college, because in college not every student will take math classes, and there are resources available to use, such as dictionaries. People majoring in literature or history might only take one math class in college since it is not relevant to their degree, so should their math SAT scores matter in the college admissions process? If a student is not considering a career in an area that requires math skills, then their math SAT scores do not demonstrate to what degree they will succeed in college. In the verbal section, students are asked to know the meanings of words that are not used in everyday conversation; in college, students are allowed to use dictionaries when writing and are thus put at a disadvantage on the SAT when such resources are not available. Just because a student memorized some words that they will likely never use or remember again does not mean that they will be able to write a convincing essay in college.

In addition, the SAT requires teenagers to be awake and to concentrate for a few hours early on a Saturday morning with only two short breaks. Most teenagers I know can barely sit through a forty-five minute class without drifting off into other thoughts at least once. This test misrepresents the situations and skills needed in college, because not only are students given more time to complete assignments and required to sit and concentrate for less time, but they also have resources available for research use. Skills that are more useful in college than answering multiple-choice questions are the abilities to do meaningful research and interpret material, and neither of these can be, nor will be, tested on the new SAT.

Some students choose to buy tutoring services or SAT prep books in hopes of improving and achieving higher scores. The attitudes that these test prep options propose are very positive, believing that "you might not be smart, but you can get lucky" (Grimes). If this test is about luck and chance, then how is it really testing our ability to do well in college? After your tutor or SAT prep book explains the format of the test and the equations you should know, they start to explain the ways to "infiltrate the mind of the Educational Testing Service"—in other words, ways for you to avoid actually knowing the material (Grimes). The SAT is supposed to help colleges compare students across the country in a standardized format, but if the test has become just a matter of working around the multiple-choice questions, then there is no purpose in using it to assess students at all.

Further, when some students are informed of these testing techniques, while others are not because they don't have the financial means or resources, the test is biased in favor of more affluent students. The changes made to the test in no way prevent this bias, because more financially sound students can still pay for help on the SATs. The only way to prevent this unfair advantage is make the only study tools available to students free and readily available to all test takers. Any other study book or tutor that requires payment would have to be prohibited under all circumstances. This rule would never come into play, though, because the College Board and other businesses make so much money off students who are willing to pay for test prep. They would be unwilling to prohibit these services and would be impossible to regulate.

Since no matter how many times the SAT is changed, it will never be an excellent assessment of how a student will perform in college, I propose that colleges and universities come to the consensus that the SAT will be a minor part of the application, and that other forms of assessment, such as AP or IB scores, that show a strong understanding of specific areas of interest be given more weight. The problem with the SAT stems not only from the College Board, but also from the colleges and universities that continue to use the SAT as a definitive part of their applications. These institutions have power over the College Board because if they decide not to use the SAT, then the College Board will be dissolved. Therefore, colleges and universities can demand more from the College Board and can work together to devise a better system of evaluation.

Works Cited

Clewell, Beatriz and Bernice Anderson. "Women of Color in Mathematics, Science and Engineering." *Center for Women Policy Studies*: 1991. Lexis Nexis. University of Colorado at Boulder, University Libraries. 13 Nov. 2004. <http://libraries.colorado.edu>.

Engelberg, Dov and Sandy Frank. "The New SAT Won't Test Students' Sanity." *Los Angeles Times*. 31 Jul. 2004: B19. Lexis Nexis. University of Colorado at Boulder, University Libraries. 6 Nov. 2004. <http://libraries.colorado.edu>.

Fitzsimmons, William. "Emphasis on Teaching Writing." *Boston Globe.* 26 Sep. 2004: D10. Lexis Nexis. University of Colorado at Boulder, University Libraries. 13 Nov. 2004. <http://libraries.colorado.edu>.

Glaberson, William. "U.S. Court Says Awards Based on S.A.T.'s Are Unfair to Girls." *New York Times.* 4 Feb. 1989. Lexis Nexis. University of Colorado at Boulder, University Libraries. 13 Nov. 2004. <http://libraries.colorado.edu>.

Grimes, William. "Ignorance Is No Obstacle." *New York Times.* 7 Nov. 2004: A4. Lexis Nexis. University of Colorado at Boulder, University Libraries. 13 Nov. 2004. <http://libraries.colorado.edu>.

Henriques, Piper. "College Board to Launch a New SAT in March." *Richmond Times-Dispatch.* 10 Oct. 2004: S13. Pro Quest. University of Colorado at Boulder, University Libraries. 1 Nov. 2004. <http://libraries.colorado.edu>.

"New SAT May Remove Cultural Bias in Test." *New Pittsburgh Courier,* Aug. 2002, Vol. 93 Issue 70, pA6. Academic Search Premier. Ebsco Host. University of Colorado at Boulder, University Libraries. 13 Nov. 2004. <http://libraries.colorado.edu>.

Argument
Sample Essay 3

WRTG 1250
Instructor: Don Wilkerson

> In his argument, David criticizes Bush's proposed guest worker program
> by comparing it to similar programs in Europe. By describing the flaws
> in existing European programs, David casts doubt on the success of
> Bush's proposal—a strategy that appeals to the reader's sense of logic.

Flaws in Bush's Guest Worker Program

DAVID HAYES

> *Give me your tired, your poor,*
> *Your huddled masses yearning to breathe free,*
> *The wretched refuse of your teeming shore.*
> *Send these, the homeless, tempest-tost to me,*
> *I lift my lamp beside the golden door!*

Long taken as the very motto of American immigration policy,
the last lines of Emma Lazarus's "The New Colossus," inscribed
beneath the Statue of Liberty, are now more relevant than ever. As
more and more people join the debate on illegal immigration, the United
States faces an interesting dilemma. Does it send these immigrants
away, violating our immigrant tradition, or allow them legal residency
with only modest penalties? Increasingly, policies appear to look toward European immigration models rather than the idealized "one great
period of immigration," as President Bush called the turn-of-the-century
period "[in which] our nation received some 18 million men, women and
children from other nations" (White House). Surely America's idealized
view of its immigration past is just that, but it seems a far better basis for
immigration policy than the Europeans programs that have recently and
blatantly shown their failings. By advocating a guest worker program
that seems far more European than American, Bush puts our country at
risk of increasing immigrant dissatisfaction and alienation in the absence
of traditional assimilation and understanding. This is made all the more
clear if we examine the failures of European immigration plans and the
successes of America's idealized immigration mythology.

Where the Bush program first errs is that it borrows heavily from Europe, where immigration policies have largely failed to produce happily
assimilated immigrants. As Fareed Zakaria, editor of *Newsweek International*, points out, "Many Americans have become enamored of the

European approach to immigration—perhaps without realizing it. Guest workers... are a part of Europe's mode of dealing with immigrants" (39). He explains why this is problematic by saying, "Across Europe one sees disaffected, alienated immigrants, ripe for radicalism" (39). Zakaria is claiming that Bush's guest worker program would be inherently flawed, and that those flaws are readily apparent across Europe today. This tells us that we must tread carefully in this debate. If indeed Zakaria is right about the similarities, these claims should worry supporters of the program. If Zakaria is right, we have good reason to avoid mimicking this approach in solving our own immigration problems.

The flaws of European guest worker programs are pointed out by Stephen Castles, a sociologist now of Oxford University. Castles argues that these workers, who were first hired after WWII, were largely made into permanent ethnic minorities who never returned home. He goes so far as to say that "guest-worker systems *inevitably* lead to permanent migration in the long run, and... it is better to plan for orderly settlement" (Castles 761). By ignoring research like Castles's, Bush's program is at risk of developing the same problems that Europe has had. In turning a blind eye to this research, we're risking the creation of an unintentional pool of immigrants with few legal rights that would further exacerbate our current problems.

The devastating effects of the failures of European guest worker programs were made strikingly clear in the Parisian riots of late 2005. In a story on the riots, CBC News supports Castles, claims by pointing out that these rioters were the remnants of the guest worker waves, and that the program created large ethnic neighborhoods that showed a volatile "combination of ethnic concentration and poverty and high unemployment" (CBC) that made these young people largely dissatisfied and disconnected from the French mainstream. Thus the remnants of the French guest-worker program clearly fomented the riots of 2005. In the absence of efforts to bring these immigrants into the mainstream of French society, due to a lack of foresight on the government planners' part, Zakaria's "disaffected, alienated immigrants" were the result.

Clearly, the French program has failed, and we can see that the Bush program ignores these failures. Bush should be applauded for attempting to provide incentives for immigrants to return home. In his proposal, he offers "tax-preferred savings accounts, [which hold] money they can collect as they return to their native countries" (White House). This and his promise to "give temporary workers credit when they enter their own nation's retirement system" (White House) are hopeful, but unrealistic. These workers can likely (without specifics of these programs we can only assume) make much more than these financial incentives by over-staying their welcome and reentering the illegal workforce. This argu-ment is supported by Philip Martin, an agricultural economics professor at the University of California Davis. Martin argues that the US Bracero program, which was in effect from 1942 to 1964 and was structured simi-larly to European programs of the same era, only served to increase ille-gal immigration. He elaborates that these workers overstayed their initial welcome for economic advantage (Martin). Much the same argument is made by Tamar Jacoby, a senior fellow at the Manhattan Institute[1] who says that "the adage is true: there is nothing more permanent than a temporary worker" (Jacoby). Jacoby allows that this could be either be-cause workers have grown attached to their new home, or because they simply desire the economic advantage. In either case, the immigrants would likely be willing to break US laws in order to stay here. Clearly, the consensus appears to be that even with Bush's new incentives there is no such thing as a guest worker. And whether they'd remain behind for economic or sentimental reasons, the law would be ineffective.

Regardless of the European failures however, some have rightly taken is-sue with the guest worker program itself as "un-American," and contrary to what many believe to be America's immigrant tradition. Many char-acterize the United States as "a nation of immigrants" where a man, or woman, can become whatever he wants so long as he'll work at it. This so-called "American dream" is central to America's immigrant mythology which, however inaccurate it is, is central to the way that Americans see themselves. Further, this "American dream" has long served to unite the disparate immigrants into a single American category. This is said quite eloquently by the editors of the *New Republic*:

> There is little that is more antithetical to the American ideal than a guest worker. While there are dangers in romanticizing this country's immigrant heritage, it is an unmistakable part of the national ethos. For generations, immigrants have come to the United States in search of a better life. In the process, they often remake themselves—as Ameri-cans. Even those who are here illegally, and whom we call illegal im-migrants, can transcend that identity—or at least see their children who are born here transcend it. (*New Republic*, 11)

By shunting guest workers into a new and previously unknown category we'd be systemically denying them a reason to assimilate or strive. Where previous immigrants were encouraged to become part of the American mainstream because it was likely to afford them success, these

---

[1] The Manhattan Institute is a leading libertarian think tank, established in 1978. According to its website, "the Mission of the Manhattan Institute is to develop and disseminate new ideas that foster greater economic choice and individual responsibility."

guest workers would be eternally placed into some new limbo. They'd be alienated with no incentive to mesh with their new country or community; after all, they're just leaving in three years anyway.

Public distaste for the creation of a "permanent underclass" is illuminated by Jacoby, who reports that in focus groups conducted by the Manhattan Institute

> Democrats and Republicans alike overwhelmingly preferred the citizenship model for reasons of both principle and practicality. It might make sense initially, these voters said, to admit workers on a provisional basis. It might also make sense to create incentives for the more transient to go home at the end of their work stints. But if they worked hard, put down roots and invested in their communities, wouldn't we want to encourage them to stay? Don't we want immigrants to assimilate? Don't we want to attract the kind of hard-working, committed folks who plan for the future and invest? (Jacoby)

Clearly, this new guest worker program is not ideologically desirable, but by this report it also lacks public support. And just as the immigrants are likely not to want to leave after the three years Bush has allowed them, Americans aren't likely to be willing to force them to go either. In this atmosphere, where neither side wants the immigrants to go, it seems most likely that they would be able to stay on illegally.

Even with Bush's further promise to "increase the annual number of green cards that can lead to citizenship," he himself admits that it would still be a "difficult path" (White House). His changes to the requirements aren't elaborated, however, so we cannot know how "difficult" this path would be. Regardless, changing the requirements now seems unfair (to put it mildly). This makes his promise to make the citizenship test harder and more rigorous ironic. Bush states that "We must ensure that new citizens know not only the facts of our history, but the ideals that have shaped our history. Every citizen of America has an obligation to learn the values that make us one nation: liberty and civic responsibility, equality under God, and tolerance for others" (White House). However, at the same time that he will ensure that potential citizens are aware of these traditional American values, he'll be subverting those very values by creating a class of immigrants who, despite popular opposition, are distinctly less than equal. By denying these immigrants access to traditional American values, he's making it all the more likely that they would become like Zakaria's "disaffected and alienated immigrants" of Europe.

Clearly then, on both ideological and historical grounds, a guest-worker program is at best likely to fail. It would deny access to the mythology of immigration that has so long been sold as part of the American experience. And leaning on the evidence from Europe, we can see that despite modest improvements, Bush's program does little to solve the problem of immigrants remaining after they're no longer welcome. For these reasons, it is wise to consider the other options available to us for giving current illegals legal status.

Works Cited

Castles, Stephen. "The Guest Worker in Western Europe—An Obituary." *International Migration Review* 20.4 (1986): 761-778.

Jacoby, Tamar. "Guest Workers Won't Work." *Washington Post* 26 Mar. 2006. 8 May 2006 <http://www.washingtonpost.com/wpdyn/content/article/2006/03/24/AR2006032401719.html>.

Martin, Philip. "There Is Nothing More Permanent Than Temporary Foreign Workers." April 2001. *Center for Immigration Studies* <http://www.cis.org/articles/2001/back501.html>.

"That's Hospitality." *The New Republic.* 17 April 2006: 11-12.

"Understanding the Violence." CBC News Online. 14 Nov 2005. <http://www.cbc.ca/news/background/paris_riots/>.

White House. "President Bush Proposes New Temporary Worker Program." 7 Jan. 2004. 8 May 2006 <http://www.whitehouse.gov/news/releases/2004/01/20040107-3.html>.

Zakaria, Fareed. "To Become an American: Guest workers, penalties and deportation are all a part of Europe's method of dealing with immigrants—which has failed." *Newsweek International* 10 April 2006 <http://www.msnbc.msn.com/id/12114153/site/newsweek/>.

Argument
Sample Essay 4

WRTG 1250
Instructor: Petger Schaberg

> An important part of presenting an argument is clearly establishing
> your position on the issue. In her essay, Amy presents her claim early
> on, and then goes on to skillfully support it through her discussion of
> information gathered from a variety of credible sources. It's clear in the
> essay that Amy has a strong interest in and opinion on the topic of the
> U.S.'s policy on torture.

Torture: The Ethics of American Policy

AMY LIPPE

*The United States has traditionally been a shining city on a hill, a beacon
of freedom and democracy and to mistreat or to inflict cruel and inhumane
treatments on people I think is just something that just harms us a great deal.*
— John McCain

"Life, Liberty, and the Pursuit of Happiness" are the first and most
fundamental rights guaranteed to Americans by the Declara-
tion of Independence. The Constitution and the Bill of Rights
specify these rights, which, in a sense, mandate an ethical treatment of
all persons, regardless of religion, race, or accused guilt in a crime. It is
the job of the three branches of government—the executive, the legisla-
tive, and the judicial—to uphold these rights and exemplify them when
representing the United States to the international community. Recently,
however, the executive branch has failed to do this. The administration
of George W. Bush has abandoned fundamental American values in its
foreign policy, for reasons that are neither ethical nor justifiable, and, in
behaving unethically, has also damaged its international relationships
and the reputation of the United States as a democratic country.

The first unethical step the administration took was ignoring United Nations (UN) protocol to wage war in 2003. The UN Charter requires that
a nation must get the approval of the UN Security Council before using
force against another country, but the United States disregarded this provision and invaded Iraq without the agreement of the Security Council.
After the war in Iraq had begun, Kofi Annan, the UN Secretary General,
stated that, "From our point of view and the UN Charter point of view, it
[the US invasion of Iraq] was illegal" (Lynch). Furthermore, not only was

it illegal, but hypocritical. As a member of the UN and a superpower in the world, it is essential for the United States to act in accordance with UN laws to maintain world peace. Simply, it is wrong for any country, regardless of size, power, or excuses, to break international law.

Once in Iraq, the administration took extreme measures to find evidence that would justify the United States presence there. The administration sought to procure information about possible terrorist and insurgent activities by authorizing that certain military officials and Central Intelligence Agency (CIA) agents could use torture against detainees. A series of memos written to the White House by lawyers in the Department of Justice justified torture as a method of interrogation. Taking advantage of loopholes in the Geneva Conventions and the UN Convention Against Torture (CAT), the memos intentionally narrowed the definition of torture and did not include "administering electric shocks to their [detainees'] genitals [...] beating them, and sexually humiliating them" in practices that would constitute torture (Wendel 81).

Furthermore, the memos provided President Bush with justification for refusing to grant Prisoner of War (POW) status to persons in the custody of the United States military in Iraq in order to evade the provisions in the Geneva Conventions and CAT against torture. The Geneva Conventions protect prisoners only if they are members of a signatory of the Conventions or of a legitimate political group (Elsea "Lawfulness" 7) and CAT; the memos established that members of the Al-Qaeda terrorist organization were not privy to rights under these terms (Wendel; Silliman). Not only did this undermine international law and rules of war, but it went against traditional United States practices, which have been to extend POW status to all of its detainees regardless of their affiliations (Elsea "Lawfulness" 8; Silliman). Former president and Nobel Peace Prize winner Jimmy Carter pointed out in an interview that no other administration since the Geneva Conventions were signed, in 1949, has attempted to circumnavigate the provisions regarding human rights (Carter). Also, it disregarded a provision of CAT that obligates states to "criminalize" acts of torture (Garcia 3). These laws show that torture is regarded by the international community as a criminal activity and thus suggest that the Bush administration used, or at least supported, criminal tactics in the war in Iraq.

President Bush has defended these tactics and the war on terror by saying they are necessary to protect American freedoms; however, there is nothing American about these policies. The practice of torture is contrary to United States law. The 5th, 8th, and 14th Amendments of the United States Constitution make it a right of citizens of the United States to have a fair trial before being punished for a crime, protect them from cruel or unusual punishment, and prohibit the State from depriving citizens of "life, liberty or property." Scott Silliman, a law professor at Duke University, has pointed out that the United States:

> Whether as a nation or simply as individuals, we have always prided ourselves on submitting to the rule of law because it is the right thing to do, regardless of the actions of others [...] if we adopt the notion that the use of torture in interrogation is justified under circumstances of our construct—the notion set forth in the memoranda—we risk becoming much like those we claim to be our enemies. (Silliman 2004)

Simply put, the practice of torture is un-American and not something with which Americans anywhere in the world should be involved. By doing so, the Bush administration is exporting a set of values that are contrary to those laid out in the Constitution. The result of these un-American values is anti-American sentiment.

In response to criticism and questioning about torture, the Bush administration has also argued that granting POW status to detainees "would interfere with efforts to interrogate them, which would in turn hamper its efforts to thwart further [terrorist] attacks" (Elsea "Treatment" 6–7). President Bush has also made remarks that the United States military is succeeding in bringing democracy to Iraq, which was previously under the dictatorship of Saddam Hussein before the US invasion in 2003. Yet in spite of any reasons the Bush administration may give to justify its behavior, it is impossible to ignore that its practice is hindering US military efforts in Iraq and discrediting image of the United States abroad.

Contrary to President Bush's hopes and claims, the war in Iraq has not lowered terrorist activity: the National Intelligence Council reported that Iraq is the new training ground for terrorists (Priest 2005: A01). Instead of protecting the United States and spreading democratic values, the inhumane tactics used by the US have fostered more intense anti-American sentiment. Insurgent attacks against US troops in Iraq have increased and "appear to be motivated by opposition to perceived US rule" (Katzman 2005: 28). Clearly, the Bush administration's anti-democratic methods are not bringing democracy to Iraq.

Another sign that the war is faltering is the lack of international support it has earned. As mentioned earlier, the Security Council did not approve the invasion, and since the beginning of the war, several allies of the United States have changed their position. For example, South Korea has long been an ally of the United States, but recently began to withdraw its troops from Iraq (Katzman 38). During her December 2005 trip to Europe, Condoleezza Rice, the secretary of state under President Bush, was pounded with questions and concerns from European leaders about torture, and several European countries, including France, have never sent troops to help in Iraq (Stevenson). The 9/11 Commission has also recognized the lack of international support for US policy:

> The 9/11 Commission, apparently finding the international discord over the treatment and status of the detainees to be harmful to the U.S. effort to thwart terrorism, recommended the development of a common coalition approach toward the detention and humane treatment of captured terrorists. (Elsea "Treatment" 3)

In other words, the US is losing the war on terror and potential allies to fight it; to progress without incurring further losses, the Bush team should embrace its democratic roots.

Finally, the Bush administration's actions have resulted in diminishing its reputation. Barbara Boxer, a United States senator from California, recently pointed out that right after 9/11 the United States had the support and sympathy of countries from Cuba to France, but as a result of the war in Iraq and the reports of US torture facilities, the United States has since lost the respect of many of these countries (Boxer). This assertion has been echoed by many other political figures; President Carter pointed out that the United States has historically been the world's champion of human rights but is now being condemned by international leaders and human rights groups (Carter). There is a huge contradiction between the Constitution protecting human rights in the United States and the executive branch of the government approving the violation of those same rights, and this is clear to the international community who has begun to doubt the integrity of the United States.

President Bush and Vice-President Cheney have asserted that in order to win the war on terror, the president must be "unconstrained" (Silliman). This is possibly the least democratic goal of the administration. The United States was a result of the American colonists resisting the absolute sovereignty of the King of England; under United States law, the people, not the government, are sovereign. Furthermore, when writing the Constitution, James Madison and other participants of the Philadelphia Convention created the system of "checks and balances," which meant that each branch of government was equally powerful, and each had the right to check the another if it attempted to assert too much power (Helm). After leaving the President unchecked for four years, Congress has finally "checked" the executive branch. The Senate, recognizing the immorality of torture and need to prevent it, just passed an amendment that would close the loopholes in the law through which the Bush administration was able to justify torture. Written by Senator John

McCain, the amendment clearly defines torture and sets guidelines, for both military personnel and C.I.A. agents working outside of the United States, that echo American and international law in condemning cruel and unusual punishment. These actions will not completely repair the Bush team's damage outside of the United States, but they are first steps in showing the world that Americans still stand for justice and integrity.

Works Cited

Boxer, Senator Barbara. Interview. *The Leonard Lopate Show*. WNYC, New York. 9 Dec. 2005.

Carter, Jimmy. Interview. *Hardball with Chris Matthews*. MSNBC. 3 Nov. 2005. Transcript: <http://msnbc.msn.com/id/9903864/>.

Elsea, Jennifer K. "Lawfulness of Interrogation Techniques under the Geneva Conventions." Congressional Research Service, The Library of Congress. 27 Oct. 2005: 30.

—. "Treatment of 'Battlefield Detainees' in the War on Terrorism" Congressional Research Service, The Library of Congress. 15 Nov. 2005: 56.

Garcia, Michael, J. *Congressional Report*. 16 June 2004: 1–19.

Helm, Ruth. Professor of American Studies, University of Colorado. Lecture Notes, Sept.–Dec. 2005.

Katzman, Kenneth. "Iraq: U.S. Regime Change Efforts and Post-Saddam Governance." Congressional Research Service, The Library of Congress. 21 Nov. 2005.

Lynch, Colum. "U.S., Allies Dispute Annan on Iraq War." *Washington Post*, 17 Sept. 2004: A18.

McCain, Senator John. Interview. *The Brian Lehrer Show*. WNYC, New York. 7 Nov. 2005.

Priest, Diana. "Iraq New Terror Breeding Ground: War Created Haven, CIA Advisers Report." *Washington Post* 14 Jan. 2005: A01.

Silliman, Scott. "Troubling Questions in Interrogating Terrorists." *Duke Magazine* 90.5 (Sept.–Oct. 2004). <http://www.dukemagazine.duke.edu/dukemag/issues/091004/depgar.html>.

Silliman, Scott. Interview. *The Brian Lehrer Show*. WNYC, New York. 17 Nov. 2005.

Stevenson, Robert, and Joel Brinkely. "More Questions as Rice Asserts Detainee Policy." *New York Times* 8 Dec. 2005.

Wendel, W. Bradley. "Legal Ethics and the Separation of Law and Morals." *Cornell Law Review* 91.1 (Nov. 2005): 67–128.

Persuasion and Rhetorical Analysis
Sample Essay 1

WRTG 1250
Instructor: Petger Schaberg

> This student example comprises two pieces. In the first piece, Patricia adopts the persona of a real person in order to compose a speech directed to a real audience. In the second piece, Patricia analyzes the rhetoric she uses in her speech. Taken together, the two show some of the relationships among speaker, message, audience, and context.

Speechwriter Assignment: Part 1, The Speech

PATRICIA LEE LOMAS

Introduction: Flemming Rose, an editor of the Jyllad-Posten *(a Danish newspaper that printed inflammatory cartoons depicting the Islamic faith) speaks to an audience of American journalists, editors, and other media communications. He seeks to persuade the audience to see that censorship has replaced the freedom of speech, and that something must be done.*

I thank you all for being here. I am excited to address the ideas of media and censorship in terms of politics. As an editor, I know that some information must be cut out. Extraneous information, articles that do not necessarily fit our newspaper, *Jyllad-Posten*, and pieces that could lose us funding all fall under that category. However, the self-censorship we impose on our print is imposed only by us; it is not government censorship, and it is not media censorship under government propaganda. Our decision to print the cartoons depicting Muhammad and other aspects of the Islamic faith demonstrates our power, as a media group, to print and say what we feel needs to be seen or heard. The cartoons, especially the one of Muhammad with a bomb for a turban, did indeed create conflict and aggression from the Muslim opposition, but it also gave us an opportunity to discuss the ideas of Islam, violence, and fanaticism with our Danish Muslim communities. More unfortunate than the outraged Muslims were the seemingly uninterested America media. Your response to these cartoons—of not printing them—made me realize that it was not so much the controversial nature of the cartoons that made them unappealing to print, but the oppressing nature and fear of censorship and propaganda throughout the entire media. I am here today to discuss the issues of government propaganda and self-censorship in the media, and to persuade you that change must take place for the sake of freedom.

America has returned to censorship; just as during World War II, when images of the dead were restricted, your president has banned the images of wounded and dead in the media. Ironically, the restrictions in WWII were lifted in order to draw support for the war, whereas your president has imposed these restrictions to keep the public interested in it. Well, the irony has got to stop. Doesn't it enrage you that you cannot print pictures of the flag-draped coffins of all those courageous soldiers who gave their lives for the ideal of freedom? If you didn't realize it before, think about it now: The media have become puppets of propaganda for the government's agenda. President Bush will not allow the images of the coffins to appear in media sources because he needs public approval to stay high; the images of death force the public to reconsider the consequences of war. This censorship, even in the slightest, hinders the pursuit of freedom. By allowing such censorship, the media become accustomed to the infractions committed against free speech, and continue simply because they know no other way.

Apart from propaganda, fear has a profound effect on people and often encourages unconscious self-censorship. In the media, from journalists to editors alike, it is fear, fear of the opposition, fear of losing a job, fear of death, fear of being unpatriotic, that contributes to mass censorship. I attribute the act of not publishing the Danish cartoons to this fear. But you cannot let this pervade your work, and your duty to give perspective and report on a story. Nor should this fear dissuade you from choosing a different article for a layout because it might be less financially successful. No, we must grab fear by the horns and dispose of the beast so that journalism and media communications can again have the freedom of their words and expression.

Your government created a bill called the Patriot Act, mandating cooperation with the government in the name of Patriotism. Nobody wants to be labeled unpatriotic, and so the media, out of fear of labels, avoid writing or reporting on an issue that might make them seem unpatriotic. In other words, they cooperate to such an extent that civil liberties are taken for granted and ignored. The flag-draped coffins once again exemplify this: The president's ban on these images has not been tested because the media are too afraid of the consequences. Why can't the media show the coffins of all the brave soldiers who died nobly? Isn't it important to report on issues that make people think about their actions? Your fear-imposed censorship transforms you into puppets of the government, making you the government's primary tools of propaganda. Even the name given to this war, "The War on Terror," expresses deep irony; As you report on the "War on Terror," you feed a different kind of terror, the same one that makes you cooperate with the government so easily, so readily. The role of the media in this war is a war in itself; however, the opposition, your freedom of speech, is weak, and the government is winning.

The government has a special relationship with the media, one that is, however, unbalanced; the government has been using the media in ways to benefit its agenda, but it has deeply hurt journalism. Imagine being sent out into the field, embedded with a battalion. You're hot and lonely, and the only people you really talk to are military personnel. You're dehydrated and hungry, but the only way for you to get sustenance is the military. You're tried and scared, and the only way for you to find shelter and receive protection is through the military. What do you think you will report on? The close quarters between the two can often create deep, personal, and of course biased relationships. The use of embedded reporters during this war has also created a union between government and media, two previously sworn enemies. Reporters talk to soldiers freely, whereas in the Vietnam War reporters were something to be wary of. These new relationships influence the footage that makes it to the public, but the press does not always release and show the footage depicting the realness of the war. So what is shown? Censored materials: Government-approved images, and self-censored outside perspectives. Although this helps the government by showing images of the war in Iraq, these images are decided upon in government offices, and are not a fair nor reliable account of the entire war.

Journalism has been suffering as the government offers the media an easy substitute for reporting. Media communications reflect an attitude of taking what's given, rather than searching, uncovering, and reporting the issues. This laziness has narrowed the media communications, leaving only a government-biased stance, when the media should really emphasize outside perspectives, and should exercise their privilege of free speech. Outside, non-government-biased perspectives, once reported and printed, reflect the free expression so greatly revered in the US. But outside reporters are scarce, and their articles and perspectives are even more so. Does this lack of perspective make you proud to be a journalist? Does this make you reconsider your freedoms? Does this make you want to make a change?

As savvy journalists and editors you have a choice about what to write and what to print. The government does not make this decision for you. And if it does, then you should fight it, in the name of your sacred freedom. I urge you to do what I did: take a chance and print controversial, sometimes offensive material. Print articles that offer an outside perspective on the war. Print images and ideas that are the expression of

your free speech. Like the cartoons, this material might bring about some
much needed discussion. Above all, I ask that you consider your civil
liberties, your freedom, and make your decisions with that in the back
of your mind, always. Don't let your outlet to discuss important issues
become corrupt and run-down with government ideas on censorship
and propaganda. Stand strong, and support your country's ideology of
freedom of expression through speech and press.

Speechwriter Assignment:
Part 2, Rhetorical Analysis

PATRICIA LEE LOMAS

Flemming Rose, the editor of the now infamous *Jyllad-Posten* newspaper,
in which the Danish cartoons depicting Islam were first printed, speaks
to an audience of American journalists and editors. The colloquial diction he uses creates empathy between the audience and the speaker. The
structure of the speech centers around two main images of censorship:
the ban of the flag-draped coffin images, and the embedded reporters
working in the field. I also employ rhetorical devices such as analogies,
metaphors, rhetorical questions, repetition, and parallel structure to persuade the audience to move away from a time of censorship, fear, and
propaganda, whether government or self-imposed.

The introduction to the speech highlights the speaker's ethos through
his use of words, while the ironic analogy to past censorship questions
the very basis for why censorship exists. The phrase "as an editor" draws
a connection between the audience and the speaker, and establishes,
within the first few lines of the speech, an empathetic ethos that holds
the audience's attention and elicits respect. The analogy between the
"War on Terror" and WWII use of censorship delineates the potential purpose of it. The ironic juxtaposition of lifting censorship to gain support
for a war with imposing censorship to gain support for a war makes the
latter appear unnecessary and wrong. I use irony to suggest to the audience that their views might also be wrong, through a subtle humor.

The visual image of the flag-draped coffins makes an ethical appeal
to the press and a pathos-based appeal to American pride. Within the
rhetorical question "Doesn't it enrage you that you cannot print pictures

of the flag-draped coffins of all those courageous soldiers who gave their lives for the ideal of freedom?" phrases such as "courageous soldiers" and "ideal of freedom" serve as symbols of American pride and freedom. By appealing to the emotions of the audience, I create more empathy between the speaker and audience, increasing the chance of persuasion. The speaker attempts to persuade the audience that the government is one reason for the censorship of images: "The media have become puppets of propaganda for the government's agenda." The metaphor compares the media to puppets, an image that explains that the media have no power, nor do they retain any benefit from serving as the government's tool for propaganda. The government can manipulate the media without any consequences. This metaphor serves as a warning for the audience, and might frighten them into persuasion.

Just as the first image uses pathos and ethos, the image of embedded reporters uses logos. The second-person words "you're hot and lonely ... you're dehydrated and hungry...you're tired and scared" force the audience to take the place of the embedded reporter and understand what the job entails. The following rhetorical question, "What do you think you will report on?" suggests that the audience can report only with an enormous bias towards the military. The rhetorical question directs the contrived answer, but still gives the audience a chance to think and interpret the question for themselves. This encourages persuasion, as the hearers feel as though they have come to a conclusion on their own. The parallel structure creates a fluidity and rhythm in speaking. The use of logos through the rhetorical question adds another element that the audience can grasp and believe.

Apart from the two main images of the speech, the speaker encourages the thought that fear acts as an overpowering reason for censorship. I use repetition and parallel structure within the syntax to create rhythm, which emphasizes a fluid, charismatic sound. "In the media... it is fear, fear of the opposition, fear of losing a job, fear of death, fear of being unpatriotic, that contributes to mass censorship." The emphasis on the word "fear" suggests that its pervasiveness is the reason for censorship. One must "grab fear by the horns and dispose of the beast so that...media communications can again have freedom." This metaphor, comparing fear to a dangerous beast, and human power and intelligence to the conquerer of the beast, shows the struggle between fear and human intelligence. The phrase "by the horns" suggests the confidence one needs to face fear, yet juxtaposes this idea with the vulnerability of being head-on to the beast, or fear. I create a metaphor so that the audience can see, in a more visual manner, the pervasive qualities of fear, and the confidence and vulnerability inherently attached to fighting it.

Lastly, the appeal to logos also comes from the statements and refutations of the counterargument. Within the first paragraph of the speech, the speaker presents the counterargument: "The cartoons...did indeed create conflict and aggression from the Muslim opposition." By stating the counterargument, the speaker appears confident in his argument, meaning his argument becomes more enticing in its persuasive qualities. The refutation, "but it also gave us an opportunity to discuss the ideas of Islam," demonstrates the superiority of his argument. The logical transition from the counter to the refutation is also found in another counterargument about embedded reporters later in the speech.

Through the use of rhetorical questions, parallel structure, metaphors, and analogies, I develop the speaker's voice as powerful and persuasive. The speech shows the audience the impact of censorship and propaganda with regard to fear and the government. Through these rhetorical devices, the speaker, Flemming Rose, can powerfully persuade the audience to move in the direction of free speech, and leave the times of censorship in the past.

Critical Inquiry Sample Portfolio

In some ways, this portfolio might be seen as an example of how the three primary processes involved in critical inquiry—analysis, argument, and inquiry—can work together to explore a topic in depth. This portfolio represents one writer's attempt to make sense of a confusing—indeed, terrifying—event that occurred in his own high school and to use that experience as an occasion to explore larger issues in American education and culture.

All of the samples were written by Mike Rotolo, a student in Paula Wenger's WRTG 1150 class, in response to an assignment sequence that asked students to expand the context for writing about a topic of immediate interest to them. For the first paper, students wrote a personal essay based on their own experience, observation, or perspective. For the next two papers—an annotated bibliography and an academic paper—students identified an issue from their personal essays to explore further through research. The final assignment was a civic essay on another issue drawn from the personal and academic papers or a variation on the issue explored in the academic paper, written for a particular publication with a definable audience. Based on the student's personal perspective, informed and shaped by research, the civic essay presented an argument on the issue to a nonacademic audience. This assignment sequence was designed to take students through the process of using academic sources and skills to deepen personal experience for the purpose of contributing more effectively to work and civic communities beyond the academy.

Personal Narrative

WRTG 1150
Instructor: Paula Wenger

A Day to Forget *and* Remember

MIKE ROTOLO

The noises reminded me of a brick of Black Cat firecrackers that I hear exploding every year on the Fourth of July. Even when several teachers ran in and out of my sophomore science class, I thought that some clever seniors were pulling off another prank. I even used the time when my teacher was out of the room to compare test answers

---

with a fellow classmate. It was not until the first pipe bomb exploded and several students fled into our room that I realized that this was more than a senior prank. The noises that I had thought were simple firecrackers were actually the first shots fired during the tragedy at Columbine High School on April 20, 1999.

The students who had fled into our room from the cafeteria on the first floor told us how men dressed in black and armed with shotguns were shooting people outside of the school. I still did not believe the ignorant freshman until a wounded faculty member, Dave Sanders, stumbled through our door and collapsed on the floor. Through the shrieks of my female classmates I could hear Mr. Sanders screaming in pain. He had been shot through the back of his neck and once through the back and his heart. My science teacher was instructing us to hide behind our desks because no one was sure where the shooters were, or even how many shooters there were. As we hid, our teacher scrambled to turn the television on, looking for any information regarding the chaos that had just begun. The local news told us that up to 150 of our classmates were wounded or dead, and this was 15 minutes after the first shot.

With the fire alarms and passing period bells ringing loudly, I sat behind my flipped desk, while other teachers entered our room and instructed the boys in the class to remove our shirts so that they could be used to stop the blood that spilled from Mr. Sanders's serious wounds. With the shirt barely off my back, I was lifted off my feet by my teacher and given a dry-erase board that read, "1 bleeding to death." I held the sign in the window, fearful that I myself would be a target for one of the shooters, while several local news helicopters flew in to film the message. After being spotted by a crouching police officer, I once again retreated behind my flipped school desk. From the phone inside our room, the police told us that they would have Mr. Sanders and the rest of us out of the classroom in 20 minutes, but the screams coming from our wounded teacher lasted for four and a half hours.

Several of my classmates led us in prayer, but the cries of pain silenced every one of us over and over. Some of the students began to show Mr. Sanders pictures of his daughters, telling him that his three beautiful girls were just one of many reasons why he had to live, and to hold on for the paramedics for one more minute.

I wanted to believe that the paramedics would be there in one minute, but 11:30 a.m. turned to 2:00 p.m., which then turned to 4:15 p.m. With each passing minute I began to feel more and more frustrated and angry, while previous worries about the destruction that had been taking place in my school began to numb away. When the S.W.A.T. unit finally arrived, the time was 4:21 p.m.—five hours after the first shot had been fired. For five hours I wondered if any of my friends had been wounded, or worse yet, killed. I thought of all the parents outside of the school who did not know if their child, their baby, had been shot or killed in the school that day.

When the door to our classroom was kicked in, a fear like I have never experienced filled every cell of my body. I wasn't sure if these men in black were the S.W.A.T. team or the killers, but a giant shield that read Denver PD settled all of our hearts. They told us that we would all be fine, and that Mr. Sanders would be taken to a hospital as soon as possible. That moment of security lasted only a second because as we were led from the classroom we heard the weak breath of our wounded teacher scream, "Tell my girls I love them." At the time it did not strike me, but I was later told that those would be Mr. Sanders's last words. We were brought from our classroom and for the first time saw the damage that had been done.

Broken glass, bullet holes, blood-stained carpet, a flooded cafeteria, bullet shells, and even our murdered classmates are what we passed as we were led out of the school at gunpoint by police officers. We were all suspects since the shooters were students. Anyone of us could have pulled the trigger, changed clothes, and fled into a classroom, even me. But the thought of who would do such a thing flopped over and over in my mind.

I felt the tears well up in my eyes when I saw my mom waiting for me at the park next to our school. My helplessness must have been evident from first sight because my mother scooped my 180-pound body up in her arms as if I were a newborn child and held me tighter than she ever has. I wanted to tell her that I wasn't scared, and that I would be fine, but I was worried about Mr. Sanders and all of my friends.

My mother told me that I was the last of my friends to exit the school and that the majority of the 2,400 students who attended Columbine had escaped within five minutes of the first shot. I also learned that one of my friends, Matthew Kecter, had been murdered that day, along with eleven other students and Mr. Sanders.

I cried with my friends for days. They wouldn't stop hugging me. We sat perplexed staring into each other's puffy eyes asking questions that we knew had no answers. Sitting in my basement with all of my friends seemed to be our only escape from chaos, our only safe haven. I remember listening to my friend Jon tell us that we needed to live every day like it was our last, and that our fear and confusion would be diminished as long as we helped one another through our times of need. It was then that I realized how precious life truly is and that each of us needed to live our lives to the fullest, for ourselves and for those whose lives were stolen from them during the tragedy. I miss my friend and I will never forget the events that happened that day in my life.

Critical Inquiry Sample Portfolio
Inquiry (Annotated Bibliography)

WRTG 1150
Instructor: Paula Wenger

Violence and Education: An Annotated Bibliography

MIKE ROTOLO

Addington, Lynn Andrea. "The Columbine Effect: The Impact of Violent School Crime on Students' Fear of Victimization." *Dissertation Abstracts International Section A: Humanities and Social Sciences*, Dec. 2002.

Addington discusses the fear of victimization experienced after Columbine by other students around the nation. This article uses polls to gather responses on the impact of Columbine in the categories of students' fear, protective behavior, and changes in school security. The author also uses the National Crime Victimization Surveys as the basis for much of her study.

This article makes good use of surveys to find the effects on students who have not witnessed a violent act firsthand, but who are still affected by the violence seen elsewhere. This article also gives brief information regarding what actions some schools are taking to prevent such events.

Arman, John. "In the Wake of Tragedy at Columbine High School." *Professional School Counseling* 3.3 (Feb. 2000): 218–20.

Author John Arman briefly explores the most common causes that are associated with violence among America's youth. He looks at topics ranging from violence in the media to violent video games and movies. Arman also discusses which of these theories have been the most popular and why.

Arman's article gives me the most popular and least popular reasons that people have come up with as to why students in schools are becoming violent. Although Arman does not go into great detail, he gives a wide range and understanding of the different theories.

Bender, William, Phillip McLaughlin, and Terresa Shubert. "Invisible Kids: Preventing School Violence by Identifying Kids in Trouble." *Intervention in School & Clinic* 37.2 (Nov. 2001): 105–11.

This article aims to inform the reader of ways to identify adolescents who have the potential for violent outbursts. The authors look closely at the shootings at Columbine High and Heritage High and cover issues spanning from bullying all the way to gun control.

From this article I was able to find information regarding how the weapons in each of the cases were obtained, as well as many determining factors in why each of the killers acted so violently.

Quinnan, Timothy. "Preparing for the Moment When a Student's Rage Turns to Violence." *Chronicle of Higher Learning* 45.49 (13 Aug. 1999): B7.

This article discusses the cause of violence among students in schools around the United States. The author uses experiences with students before and after tragedies to explore the cause and effect of such events as Columbine High. This article also looks at possible ways to prepare schools and universities for school shootings or other traumatic incidents.

This article examines many different causes for violence in schools at both a high school and college level. It also briefly touches on effects on students and ways to cope and prevent similar situations.

Soskis, Benjamin. "Bully Pulpit." *New Republic.* 14 May 2001: 25–27.

Author Benjamin Soskis focuses on bullying as a factor influencing adolescents to act violently. He explores the differences between the students who bully and the students who are bullied. Soskis also looks at different factors that might make a violent combination if added to being bullied.

"Bully Pulpit" gives me detailed information about what type of children bully and why they do it. This article also looks at how to identify those who are bullied and also how to identify children who seemed troubled by isolation.

Ulschmid, Nancy. "The Psychological Consequences of Community Violence Exposure: What Variables Protect Children in Urban Settings?" *Dissertation Abstracts International Section A: Humanities and Social Sciences*, Feb. 2002.

The author studies 121 students, ages 11–15, who have been exposed to violent acts while attending public schools. She analyzes effects ranging from disabilities to stress and anxiety syndromes. This study also looks at the difference in the effect of violent acts on boys and girls.

This article will provide data taken from students who have witnessed a violent act to analyze several effects. This article gives both demographics that had little effect and those that had a greater effect.

Critical Inquiry Sample Portfolio
Inquiry

WRTG 1150
Instructor: Paula Wenger

Eliminating Violence and Trauma

MIKE ROTOLO

As newspaper headlines more frequently involve violence or violent acts and the top story on a local news station is a report about a murder, one may start to wonder why this sort of violence is showing up in classrooms and schools everywhere. There are many beliefs and theories on why violence in schools is becoming more common, but in the wake of such tragedies as Columbine High School in Littleton, Colorado, and Heritage High in Conyers, Georgia, many ideas about causes, as wells as effects, of these acts of violence become seemingly more evident. Regardless of the number of victims or severity of violent acts in schools, the classroom simply has no place for such behavior, and many new methods aim to diminish it. By addressing what causes students to act so violently toward one another, schools will be able to prevent violence before it occurs and eliminate lifelong scars, whether physical or emotional, that come from witnessing a violent act. With this better understanding of our students as both perpetrators and victims of violent acts, parents, teachers, counselors, and principals will possess the knowledge it takes to operate an environment of learning, understanding, and responsibility.

The most common question that can barely be understood through the rivers of tears that stream down the faces of students, teachers, and family members alike when dealing with a traumatic experience is why? Why did they do it? Why our school? Scholars all over the world look for these answers every time violence and schools mix together. Many point the finger at the "darker dimensions of popular culture, such as violent video games and movies, 'gangsta' rap music, and misanthropic World-Wide Web sites and chat rooms" (Quinnan 1). In many cases, the entire American culture, most importantly the media, is being examined and also blamed for many of the violent outbursts that are revealing themselves in our nation's schools.

As entertainment industries make billions of dollars a year selling sex, violence, and action to fan bases reaching nearly every inch of the United States, many are questioning the effect that this may be having on our nation's youth. Even musicians such as Marilyn Manson and other rock stars who stray away from the MTV norm are being accused of making music that provokes violence and anger in young Americans. However, many believe that the violence and anger that are often depicted in music videos, movies, and television shows are not affecting the actual perpetrators of these violent acts seen in schools; instead it is provoking some students to harass and bully their peers who are seen as different. As scholars begin to investigate different causes for America's violent culture, the most common reason offered is that the "bully" is now "the embodiment of a youth culture so cruel that it leads the persecuted to kill" (Soskis 1). In other words, being mocked or mistreated by a peer for whatever reason causes these already emotionally hurt students to snap. Although seventy-five percent of adolescents admit to being bullied and five million elementary and junior high students are bullied each year, many still believe that bullying, despite how common it is, combined with certain personality traits, can be a mixture for an act of violence (Bulach, Fulbright, Williams 1). Still, many wonder why being bullied can push some students to the point of murder and often suicide when more than three quarters of American adolescents experience bullying. The latest acts of violence seen in Colorado and Georgia reveal startling similarities in traits that are found in all of the perpetrators. The first is that each of the white males, T.J. Solomon in Georgia and Dylan Klebold and Eric Harris in Colorado, demonstrated indicators to peers of emotional problems and a low regard for life. Other similarities include alienation from family and friends, warnings given to others in advance by talking about killing someone, average or above-average intelligence, and *deliberate* actions on the day of the shooting (Bender, McLaughlin Shubert 2). Each of these factors can be combined with the experience of being bullied, or picked on, to generate many scenarios that might be the reason for these violent acts.

The most important of these factors that might create the combination for violence when added to being bullied are emotional factors. T.J. Solomon, the shooter in Georgia, had been under medical treatment for depression, and one of the shooters from Colorado, Eric Harris, was described as a troubled teen who was suffering from obsession and depression (Bender, McLaughlin, Shubert 2). The mixture of the bullying and the depression creates alienation from not only family and friends, but also from the larger school community. This depression and constant battering of self-esteem generates itself into an eventual lowering or declining respect for life. This cycle and disregard for life is especially exemplified in the actions of Klebold and Harris, by the statements of dissatisfaction they made both before and during the shooting, and also by the vast number of victims. By ruthlessly killing whoever they could, Klebold and Harris demonstrated their lack of care and respect for their victims' lives, and by killing randomly they proved their alienation from the entire school community by showing hatred for all. These internal behaviors are often manifested from being picked on by more aggressive students and are evident in prior warnings that went unnoticed: "Prior to the Columbine Shooting, a video made by Harris and Klebold for a video production class showed the boys acting out a scene that involved anger, violence, and revenge" (Bender, McLaughlin, Shubert 2). Solomon too showed his true feelings when "following the breakup with his girlfriend he became angry and spoke of suicide and bringing a gun to school." Solomon also told two classmates that he had no reason to live and that he would blow up the classroom, and this just one day prior to the shooting (Bender, McLaughlin, Shubert 2). With underlying emotions of negativity and depression, the only escape from the relentless torment and humiliation caused by being bullied was an act of violence, carried out by hatred and with cruelty.

Despite the popularity of the belief that school bullies pushed the already troubled teens to their breaking point, still others believe in and insist on other causes of school violence. Many believe that if guns were not so accessible in our society, violent and potentially deadly acts would be non-existent in classrooms and in schools. The Tec-DC9 semiautomatic firearm used by Klebold and Harris at Columbine was purchased by a friend at a gun show, and then given to them. Also, Klebold's girlfriend admitted to "buying a Hi-Point semiautomatic carbine and two 1969 Savage shotguns," (Bender, McLaughlin, Shubert 2), all of which were used during the massacre. The weapons used by Harris and Klebold were the first used in a string of school shootings where the guns were actually purchased. Accessibility to guns also helped Solomon execute his plan because he was able to take guns from an unlocked display case in his family's home and the ammunition needed for the weapons from a drawer underneath. In both of these cases, the accessibility of firearms helped the perpetrators unleash their fury in fatal ways. Without this easy access, the teens would have been forced to deal with their depression and anger in other ways, and although they still might have turned to violence, it would have taken place on a much smaller scale. Many believe that the availability of weapons such as guns provoke troubled teens to take the most drastic measures when coping with problems, as opposed to reaching out for help or finding another, more positive emotional outlet. Many point to other causes such as "out of touch parents, unrestricted access on the Internet to information on how to build pipe bombs, the effects of mental illness, over-burdened school counselors, lacking resources for mental health services in schools, racism, and violence in the media" (Arman 3). No matter what the cause, students are still pushed to their breaking point and violence is usually an inevitable outcome, while the cost of these outbursts is the lives of their victims and traumatic effects experienced by many.

With so many fingers pointing to different causes and putting blame on others, many rarely stop to think about the various levels and types of effects that a violent act such as a school shooting might cause. Although most acts of violence cause trauma to those who were present, tragedies like the school shootings in Colorado and Georgia had effects on students, teachers, parents, entire communities, and even the entire nation. One consequence of violent acts of this size is a feeling and fear of victimization at school among students nationwide (Addington 1). In most parts of the country, victimization felt by students was only moderate and simply increased school security, although very minimally. In towns such as Littleton and Conyers, however, different effects were present because of the magnitude of the tragedy that occurred in their schools, yet even these effects were in different forms and different levels. For example, "Children who directly experience the event face higher risk than do children who witness the event from a distance" (Kirk 1). Already, two different risk levels are set up simply by an adolescent's location or involvement in the actual event. For those who simply witness the act from a distance, a feeling of victimization will again be present, but survivor's guilt also emerges because of relationships with those who were directly involved, either as close witnesses or victims. Although some will experience different levels, most of the students and school personnel who witnessed Columbine "have suffered from survivor guilt, anger, overwhelming grief, and essentially post-traumatic stress syndrome" (Arman 1). Of these symptoms, the most common and the symptom with the greatest risk of disabling the life of a person is post-traumatic stress disorder (PTSD).

Many people with PTSD repeatedly re-experience the ordeal in the form of flashback episodes, memories, nightmares, or frightening thoughts, especially when they are exposed to events or objects reminiscent of the trauma. Common side effects usually result in the witness experiencing emotional numbness and sleep disturbances, depression, anxiety, and irritability or outbursts of anger. Post-traumatic stress disorder can last a minimum of one month; however, each victim will handle his or her disorder differently, so recovery times cannot be accurately estimated.

Other problems experienced by firsthand witnesses include major depression, anxiety, and behavior problems. The side effects that are experienced by those who witnessed the violence can vary because of the gender of the adolescent, but the adolescent response also differs from the level at which adults who witnessed the tragedy are affected. Adolescent girls, for example, reported a wider range of trauma symptoms such as sensation-seeking, atypicality, somatization, social stress, and inadequacy that most boys do not encounter (Ulschmid 1). The differences in effects caused by a violent act is also different than that of adults. Adults or teachers, who are obviously much older, have had a life full of experience and thus are equipped to deal with their emotions on a much more rational level. Although these effects may be on the same level as the students, "adolescents are particularly at risk because of issues surrounding identity formation, self esteem, and developmental differences in coping mechanisms" (Kirk 1). For these reasons, an adult will handle his or her emotions better due to experience, whereas adolescents and young teens are still trying to find themselves and still experiencing new emotions. Although emotions such as survivor guilt, anger, and victimization are usually short-term effects, many witnesses, regardless of gender and age, will experience trauma for a long period of time. Feelings of anxiety, depression, and PTSD will often stay with individuals until they confront the symptoms, which are often prolonged because of denial. Although the long-term effects of witnessing an act of violence such as school shootings are still being studied, it is known that experiencing such an event can be traumatic for long periods of time and can even be life altering. As school violence such as the events in Littleton and Conyers begins to become more common, many people are now focusing their attention on how to prevent these acts from happening by reaching these troubled teens before they act out in desperation.

Initially, the idea of preventing these horrible acts of violence seemed very clear. Identify the children who are in and out of the principal's office because of their bullying, aggressive behavior, or other conduct disorders (Bender, McLaughlin, Shubert 3). These externalizing behaviors that are displayed by these students are immediately noticed by their teachers, and they are identified as potential violent students. However, as school violence seems to be more frequent, evidence is proving that these "aggressive students" are not actually the perpretrators of school violence. Instead, the "students who are easiest to ignore are using violence to offset and counteract their anonymity" (Bender, McLaughlin, Shubert 3). These students have internalized their aggression, as opposed to the more common externalizaton, and it results in an explosion of violence. With these astounding new findings, new ways of identifying teens who are potentially violent are being developed.

After finding that the students responsible for the recent tragedies in many schools were virtually unknown to many school officials prior to the shooting incidents, many schools implemented Warning List and Profiling to identify all students. Although this was an effective way to track children with previous violent outbursts, it was still very difficult to identify those who might potentially act out. Problems with the Warning List method of profiling students arise very frequently because it is "dependent on the teachers' knowledge of the emotional well being of all the students in their class" (Bender, McLaughlin, Shubert 4). This poses huge problems when trying to observe troubling behavior because those students who are internalizing their aggression will not display any violent or anger-driven traits externally. The problems with this method of identifying potentially violent teens were demonstrated by the shootings at Columbine and Heritage High Schools when all three perpretrators were not students recognized as being troubled or showing previous aggressive behavior. In the light of these new findings, other methods of prevention look to peers, not teachers or school officials, to help identify troubled teens before they lash out.

After efforts by teachers to clearly identify troubled teens in their classes failed, many findings suggest that the most effective "set of eyes and ears in the school building are the students" (Bender, McLaughlin, Shubert 5). When looking at the most recent school shootings that have taken place in the United States, researchers note that teachers and principals had no concern about the students' behavior, but other students knew that something was not right. Countless interviews after the shooting at Columbine High School were filled with students speaking of the Trench Coat Mafia, the violent writings of the perpretrators, and their isolation from other students within the school. However, when officials at Columbine were asked about the information that was given by so many students, they told reporters that they had not previously heard about these things. For reasons such as this, many schools are turning to peer screening as a method to identify teens who are troubled. By using a rating system, teens rate every student in their class on several statements.

Statements such as, "I would like to sit next to this person at lunch" are rated a scale ranging from 1–5, one being strongly agree and five being strongly disagree. After students' scores are tabulated and averaged, teachers can easily identify students who have few friends and therefore may be likely candidates for dissociation from others in the school environment. As this method becomes more popular, analysis shows that not only does this help in identifying those students with few social contacts, but it also allows teachers to implement formal and informal interventions to assist in the developement of socially isolated children (Bender, McLaughlin, Shubert 5). Clearly the Peer Screening method of identifying and preventing possible acts of violence is taking a step in the right direction. However, even this technique might soon present some flaws in the wake of the next act of extreme school violence.

Whether looking for answers to the cause of school violence, analyzing the traumatic effects that it causes in adolescents, or even attempting to prevent it, the extreme violence that has recently popped up it schools in the United States has gathered global attention. Many still blame the aggressive American culture that children are submerged in from birth, while others point the finger at school bullies. Any way you look at it, tragedies like those at Columbine High School and Heritage High School have magnified the problem of troubled adolescents and the ability to deal with pressures of growing up and life at school. By studying the behavior of both perpratrators and victims alike, we can have a better understanding of both how to identify and prevent these acts of violence, and also deal with and help eliminate side effects that might emerge from witnessing an act of extreme violence.

Works Cited

Addington, Lynn Andrea. "The Columbine Effect: The Impact of Violent School Crime on Students' Fear of Victimization." *Dissertation Abstracts International Section A: Humanities and Social Sciences*, Dec. 2002.

Arman, John. "In the Wake of Tragedy at Columbine High School." *Professional School Counseling* 3.3 (Feb. 2000): 218–20.

Bender, William, McLaughlin, Phillip, and Shubert, Terresa. "Invisible Kids: Preventing School Violence by Identifying Kids in Trouble." *Intervention in School and Clinic* 37.2 (Nov. 2001): 105–11.

Bulach, Clete, Fulbright, Penland, and Williams, Ronnie. "Bullying Behavior: What Is the Potential for Violence at Your School?" *Journal of Instructional Psychology* 30.2 (June 2003): 156–64.

Quinnan, Timothy. "Preparing for the Moment When a Student's Rage Turns to Violence." *Chronicle of Higher Learning* 45.49 (13 Aug. 1999): B7.

Soskis, Benjamin. "Bully Pulpit." *New Republic*. 14 May 2001: 25–27.

Ulschmid, Nancy. "The Psychological Consequences of Community Violence Exposure: What Variables Protect Children in Urban Settings?" *Dissertation Abstracts International Section A: Humanities and Social Sciences*, Feb. 2002.

Critical Inquiry Sample Portfolio
Argument

WRTG 1150
Instructor: Paula Wenger

Violence at Columbine: Why?

MIKE ROTOLO

Note: *I am writing this piece for* Newsweek's *section called "My Turn." This will give me an opportunity to reach people of all backgrounds, knowledge of the events, and ages. I think that leaving this open to a broad range of audiences is the best way to approach an article that covers a topic that affected the entire country, and even world.*

Many different theories have been generated since the school shooting at Columbine High School, in Littleton, Colorado, on April 20, 1999. Some of these theories revolve around violence in the media, bad parenting, and even violent video games. However, the two theories that have sparked the most controversy put the blame on bullying and isolation, or on easy access to guns. Many believe that the combination of bullying and easy access to guns was the determining factor in prompting Dylan Klebold and Eric Harris to such violent rage on their fellow classmates that day. Still, a closer look at what really took place at Columbine High School prior to the shootings seems to reveal a different story than what was portrayed on the news worldwide.

I was a sophomore at Columbine when the tragic shooting that took the lives of thirteen students and one faculty member startled the world.

At first many began to put the blame on bullying. For most people the theory that "bullies" had driven these already emotionally unstable teens to snap seemed very rational and probable. Yet, I, along with many other Columbine students and faculty members, was left more confused and dumbfounded than ever. The confusion did not stem from the theories themselves, but from the claims made regarding which students, and which types of students, were involved with either end of the bullying.

With an astounding "seventy-five percent of adolescents admitting to being bullied and five million elementary and junior high students being bullied each year," it would be unrealistic to say that bullying did not take place at Columbine High School (Bulach, Fulbright, Williams 1). As a student at Columbine, I witnessed different levels of bullying, and the most severe forms rarely, if ever, involved the students who would later murder their fellow classmates and teacher. The most severe and aggressive bullying was aimed toward athletes by other athletes. Just like in all levels and types of athletics, new team members are often picked on as a rite of passage, or as a way to distinguish the freshmen teams from the junior varsity teams, and the junior varsity from the varsity teams. Being a football player, I saw and received bullying from older athletes, not because we were different or because they disliked us and wanted to humiliate us, but instead because it is natural for the older students to seek dominance and power over the younger students. Although one might speculate that these acts of bullying may isolate the athletes who are receiving the bullying, they actually somewhat initiate the athlete into the larger family of athletes who make up all levels of the sport, freshman through varsity. By no means am I condoning or supporting these bullying rituals and vicious cycles that are found in high schools all over the country, but I do question the theory that bullying was the main reason that Dylan Klebold and Eric Harris chose to murder.

Both were members of the Trench Coat Mafia, a group of more than ten Columbine students who wore black trenchcoats to school daily. Neither Klebold nor Harris was isolated from the entire student population. In fact, a picture and letter at the end of the 1998 and 1999 school yearbook showed the group of friends together and talked about all the fun times they had shared over the past year. At the same time, neither of the students participated in school sports, so neither would have been subjects of the bullying that takes place to initiate younger athletes. What then, if not bullying or isolation, made these two students want to kill? Although there is no definite answer to this very touchy question, I believe that an interest in violence and guns generated from idealizing Adolf Hitler, combined with easy access to guns, not bullying, drove these students to kill.

Both Klebold and Harris demonstrated their interests in violence when a video made "for a video-production class showed the boys acting out a scene that involved anger, violence, and revenge" (Bender, McLaughlin, Shubert 2). In addition, videos recently released by the Jefferson Country Sheriff's Department show the two killers taking target practice at human-shaped targets, thus revealing their fascination with guns and destruction. Although their attraction to guns played a huge role in the violent nature of the two killers, the easy access to these guns helped them turn their violent video-production project into a reality.

Many believe that if guns were not so accessible in our society, violent and potentially deadly acts would be nonexistent in classrooms and schools. The Tec-DC9 semiautomatic firearm used by Klebold and Harris at Columbine was purchased by a friend at a gun show, and then given to them. Also, Klebold's girlfriend admitted to "buying a Hi-Point semiautomatic carbine and two 1969 Savage shotguns," all of which were used during the massacre (Bender, McLaughlin, Shubert 2). The weapons used by Harris and Klebold were the first used in a string of school shootings where the guns were actually purchased. Without the weapons, Klebold and Harris would never have had the opportunity to put their violent thoughts and plans into action, thus preventing the tragedy from ever taking place. Although the fascination with guns and violence might still be present, harder access to guns would restrict this fascination from taking over the boys' lives and prevent them from acting upon their violent fantasies.

Since the shooting in April of 1999, a number of theories have been presented about what drove Dylan Klebold and Eric Harris to commit murder at Columbine High School. Of these theories, none have been examined more than bullying and easy access to guns. With so many of the United States' adolescents being bullied each year, some are starting to question why these certain few are pushed to kill, and so many are not. This is leading many to believe that other aspects such as easy access to guns, instead of bullying, is provoking students to act upon violent fantasies. As access to firearms becomes easier and easier, so is the ability to put violent plans into action. Instead of looking at who might have caused these killers to act, we should look at what outlets enable these adolescents to act on violent manifestations—in this case, the easy access to guns and firearms.

Note: For a discussion of reflection and its relationship to writing, see page 15.

Reflection
Sample Essay 1

WRTG 1100
Instructor: Michelle Albert

> Reflective writing can be a way of making sense of various thoughts and ideas that have more or less consciously influenced a writer's thinking. Will makes sense of his experience in WRTG 1100 through metaphors that help him relate his own process of writing—and dealing with writer's block—to other experiences, such as taking a run.

Reflective Essay

WILLIAM F. HOUSE

What have I learned in my writing class? And what can I say about reflecting on that? What I've learned is that writer's block can be and is one of the most foul and unpleasant things that a person can experience. However, for me, I think it's necessary. Or at least, that's what I've decided I'll let it be. Do I have it right now? No. Have I folded up like a card table at its influence before? You bet I have. I've decided this though: Write when the tide is in and soak up experience when the tide is out.

When our literary tide is in, the words flow and ideas wash up like smooth, iridescent sea glass. We're buoyed up by this ocean of words and you can't help but write; the sentences are just *there*. And they come out with little to no prodding. Then, perhaps on a regular basis or maybe at the most inopportune times, the tide will go out. As a writer or student, we begin to panic. We panic or fret because we have a deadline or because our professors are expecting us to fulfill our assignment or because we just feel that we "should" write. We're writers, for the love of Steinbeck! Where are the words?!

I say, take a deep breath and just realize that the tide isn't gone for good; it's just *out*. And this is the perfect time to explore and soak up experience. This is the time that real writers emerge. They go down and wade out onto the tidal flats and see what lives in the tidal pools. They take in the pungent salt air. They notice the seastars and snails and kelp and mollusks left behind. They listen and feel. They know that their muse is like the moon, always thirsty for the ocean and pulling our words away generally more than she gives them to us (or so it seems at times).

One night a few weeks ago, I went for an evening run. It was getting dark and raining out. And, in fact, it was snowing above us in the mountains. I slipped on my running pants and a warm top and my trusty Sauconys and after a few minutes of stretching, I headed out. I ran to the end of our street and through a tunnel that goes under the road and into the park next door. It was very quiet and I had that excitement that you get at the beginning of a run where you really want to run fast, but you know you have to pace yourself. I fell into a pace that was comfortable and ran as the sun slid behind the peaks.

I generally run near Wonderland Lake and then up into the foothills. That night, as I rounded the shoreline, steam was coming off the water as the night air quickly grew cooler than the lake. The trail was nearly deserted as only a few runners passed me. We all smiled at each other like this was the best-kept secret in the whole world. The moon was nowhere to be seen and it grew quiet as I pushed up into some of the trails above the lake.

Soon, I wasn't passing anyone and my feet were growing heavier with mud. I splashed through several puddles to try and get rid of some of the unwanted stowaway dirt. Just as I topped a small hill, I looked over and noticed the warm lights of many homes in the valley as people were having dinner or maybe talking about which ski resort would open first this year. I topped the hill and began going down the other side. The city slid away and there was nothing but night and rain and the sound of breathing and feet hitting the wet soil. My mind felt as quiet as my run. I wasn't thinking about anything in particular, but I was completely lucid and more alert than I'd been all week. And for a moment, I stopped mentally and thought, This is what we need as writers: simple, but rich experience. And I thought of all the simple and sometimes profound experiences that we all go through. I thought of sitting with patients at the hospital where I work, listening to their stories and of how they're afraid to die, but happy to be alive. I thought of driving home the night before this particular run and how the clouds were lifting from the mountains and the sun was breaking through against the rocks and how I got a lump in my throat just from the sheer beauty of it. I thought of how my dad made up cowboy stories for me at bedtime for as far back as I could remember. I thought of seeing my daughter being born and having her look at me for the first time. I thought of a moment in my life enduring physical pain that was so intense that I thought I would pass out and wished I had. I thought of standing on top of the Eiffel Tower for the first time and seeing the morning sun break over Paris. I thought of sitting at my Uncle Dan's pond as a boy, fishing and getting sunburned. I thought about the first time I started an IV on someone and realized that I knew what being a doctor was like. I thought about the first time I sailed...

...and then, I was running again. I was back down near the lake. I could hear the city noises again. A young girl passed me on the trail and huffed out a quick "hey" as she went by. A man who must have been in his seventies ran by me like I was standing still and made me smile in spite of myself. And I thought, my tide may be out right now, but tomorrow I will write and let all this experience out onto the page.

Writer's block isn't bad. It's just your tide being out. If we view it in that light, a funny thing begins to happen. Before you're even ready perhaps, you'll notice the tide coming back in and pooling into your footsteps, following you back up to higher ground. And even sometimes, the tide comes back in hard and fast and just like the real ocean, it brings an abundance of life back to the shoreline. Our tide of experience can bring new life into our words and into our writing. We just have to allow it.

So, that's what I've learned this semester in my writing class, and this is the best way I know to reflect on it, to simply write it. I think I've known that my strengths are conveying something with a sense of truth and knowing how to drive home fact or elicit an emotional response. My biggest fear and insecurity in writing was simply not knowing how to deal with writer's block. Through the tools I learned in this class and from the encouragement and help of my instructor (and peers), I've learned that I can deal with the issue, though. The class and the lesson have been helpful and important to me in ways that exceed the scope of the class.

All of this reminds me of a favorite line from a Tom Hanks film called *Castaway*. There's a scene where he's describing the incredible hardship of being stranded for years on an isolated island and of the unexpected good fortune he receives. He says, "Tomorrow the sun will rise. Who knows what the tide could bring?" My writing has changed in light of that. It's just like my life; there will be good times and not so good times, but we just keep trying.

Reflection
Sample Essay 2

WRTG 1250
Instructor: Rolf Norgaard

> Rules. Like many accomplished young writers, Caroline Bess was well acquainted with the standard grammatical and stylistic tyrannies, not to mention the individual quirks and obsessions of her teachers. For her final project, Caroline reflects on the role of rules in writing. To what extent do they enable or constrain? And how much "[s]hould we as a society lighten up or buckle down?"
>
> In this essay, Caroline weaves reflection, personal narrative, analysis, inquiry, and argument into her discussion of the rules of language. While this is not a typical reflective essay, Caroline's writing demonstrates how reflecting on the writing process might be connected to a broader inquiry into controversies about language use in our culture.

The Rules

CAROLINE BESS

On the first day of seventh grade, I was sitting down among the faces of the future, waiting expectantly to meet yet another teacher who would have a hand in my intellectual molding, when I saw the sign that would set the tone for my academic career. It said, "Got is Gone." The big red letters on the white tagboard seemed almost as imposing as my teacher's huge, domineering stature as he walked to the front of the classroom to introduce himself. Both the sign and the man had a certain boldness that demanded deference, prohibited skepticism. I did not have to wait long to learn that the sign meant we were not to use any variation of the word got. And if we were to use the forbidden word in our writing, our assignment would be penalized one letter grade—that's how serious he was about it.

My teacher had brilliantly boiled down the art of writing to a single rule by which to gauge our progress. In fact, he often didn't even have to read the assignment. He was a certified speed-reader who could scan an entire essay in seconds, and, wielding his mighty pen, strike out every *got* he saw obstructing his path. And now, as I reflect back on my early education, most memories grow hazy, but I will always remember watching as he graded my semester project in one minute flat. I grew increasingly dismayed as he eradicated one, two, three variations of *got*. Just like that, I had gotten a "C." And let me tell you, I'll never use that word again.

This early display of grammatical tyranny was the first of many unyielding language rules to come that would reveal an excessively narrow view on the ills of modern American writing. The academic elitism that promotes a constricted focus on nit-picky rules serves as blinders to the degeneration of articulate and expressive writing. The ultimate goal of functional literacy, let alone literary art, falls by the wayside as the path is obstructed by grammatical dogma. What is the point of perfect structure if a phrase has no force? From my seventh grade take-off point, I was to encounter teachers who would drill into my head ranting oaths about countless grammatical laws, like "never ever, under any circumstances, will the passive voice be used" and "You'll forever abstain from using contractions in your writing." And really, where would I be if it weren't for this word orthodoxy keeping me in line? Surely, I would have been swept away by a swift river of grammatical travesties into a great pool of societal decadence from which this collapse of language spawns. I would have become just another base perpetrator of this "creeping casualness" that so many linguists, teachers, and moralistic grammar police are up in arms about (Eakin).

And what exactly are these conservatives up in arms about? Well, specifically, the "poor grammar, sloppy syntax, misused words, misspelled words, and other infelicities of style" that they see in their colleagues', students', and leaders' writing ("Clues to Concise Writing"). It is they who write enraged letters to the editors for allowing grammatical lapses as if they were moral travesties. William Safire, a self-proclaimed enforcer of proper speech, is one of the squeakiest wheels out there, notorious for his indictments of America's "sloppiness in speech," whether it's caused by "ignorance or apathy" (Safire). And one has to wonder how the moralistic tone entered the song of these "language snobs." Linguistic conservatives fear that the structures, much like grammar, that "provide our security are in danger of collapse" (Williams). Not only do they rail against the language's misuse, but they lament the impending changes of it. They scoff at the annual alterations and additions to Webster's Standard Dictionary, such as "gift" and "impact" being amended to be verbs as well as their conventional definitions as nouns.

But the very notion of defending grammar is a little childish and willful. For example, one thousand years ago in Old English, "Happy New Millennium, Everybody" would have been "Bliss on baem cumendum busend leara, Eallum!" (Kurland). No one looks at the status quo of grammar in respect to Old English and thinks, "We're such barbarians—what we've done to our forefathers' language is sacrilege!" People understand that languages, just like people and societies and thoughts, evolve. With a little perspective, it's difficult to imagine the English language had it remained static. It's futile to resist the changes in grammar that are being made today. So the current complaints about the degradation and evolution of the language are pretty myopic, really. Granted, grammatical slippages are jarring to a trained ear, and they can sometimes even be alarming, such as President Bush's comment on the educational testing system in which he says, "You teach a child to read, and he or her will be able to pass a literacy test."

However, one must question how dire poor grammar really is in the face of greater linguistic troubles. Perhaps there's a greater ill that's being overlooked by the likes of the grammar police, and that is a development of "vagueness and sheer incompetence" in the style of modern prose, as the art of style is viewed as superfluous (Orwell). Perhaps this crusade against grammar trespassers is pulling the wool over our eyes. A more pertinent issue, more significant than a misused "whom" here or an unnecessary preposition there, is how our language has become "ugly and inaccurate because our thoughts are foolish" (Orwell). To this end, a more appropriate, and more alarming, quote from President Bush might be his statement in which he fervently asserted, "I know what I believe. I will continue to articulate what I believe and what I believe—I believe what I believe is right." Articulate? I think not. Neither is it graceful nor moving, as was the style of political leaders past. Perhaps the English language is losing something more important than impeccable subject-verb conjugation.

Our American president's use of dialect nicely highlights the contentiousness between linguistic conservatives and liberals. On the one hand, if our president, one of the most powerful and influential men in the world, can perform his job in the midst of grammatical carnage, then what's the difference? In the grand scheme of things, his slip-ups are not so calamitous. And on the other hand, it is our president, one of the most powerful and influential men in the world, who is consistently breaching grammar laws. Should we as a society lighten up or buckle down? This is the question. And my own experience with teachers buckling down has helped me to come to my own answer.

My teachers' narrow catering to prescriptive grammar hampered the possibility for creative advancement in my writing. In middle school, I abided by the grammar dogma religiously, for my teachers allowed no leeway. High school was not so terribly different; I still took my oaths and listened to various English teachers berate those grammatical urchins who were still writing sentence fragments and run-ons. But this was when we started analyzing rhetorical devices and syntax strategies in masterpieces of literature. We would write perfectly formed essays, with the thesis at the end of the first paragraph, appropriately placed topic sentences, and an all-inclusive conclusion at the end, even as we were writing about unconventional stylistic strategies that have been lauded for centuries. Run-on sentences quickened the pace of one passage to convey a sense of urgency. There was improper capitalization in another to allow for greater flexibility in emphasis. Sentence fragments were a particularly potent way of accentuating a point. Switching tenses mid-piece was not careless writing—it was a deliberate and essential volta in the tone and meaning. So, we students wrote endless essays on these rhetorical devices, but I don't recall ever once being encouraged to write with the same finesse. We were trained to recognize the art that creative writing can generate, but our own expression was shackled by the commitment we had made to convention from our early education. As students, we have been taught in such a way that as we write, we have a constant dialogue of "should" and "shouldn't" that doesn't allow us liberty of expression. I think we've been buckled down too tightly.

So as the intellectual elite are now up in arms about the English language's "abuse and misuse in the news, media, and elsewhere," I find myself wondering what exactly they are aiming to salvage if we as a society are no longer capable of creating art through the language (Society for the Preservation of English). There is a plethora of societal changes that are challenging the creative beauty of writing. We are an increasingly oral-based culture, for one. We get our news through the television and radio versus the newspaper. And when we do write, instead of letters, we communicate via e-mail, in which the writing is condensed as much as possible into clips like "ur," "g2g," "ttyl," and "brb." Letter writing is no longer an art, but a skill in concision. So we, as a society, are no longer reading or writing for news, entertainment, or education. Seems to me that grammar is the least of our worries as far as the fate of the English language is concerned. (Oh dear, thank God for Microsoft Word—had my previous sentence fragment not been underlined with a squiggly green line, I know not what I'd have done. This corporation has dutifully taken upon itself the task of keeping billions of word documents within the checks of pre-ordained grammar laws. But do you know what I'm even more thankful for about Microsoft Word? The *ignore* button.)

In fact, it is even arguable that as the language evolves, and as we deviate from the diction of "privileged classes from the past," we open up a greater freedom and potential for creative expression (Nunberg). So as our standards for grammar and definition evolve along with the times, what will this new voice sound like? Will it really be the voice of slovenliness and foolishness, or will it be the voice of inventiveness and expressiveness? Or perhaps it will merely temper the haughty, condescending tone of our intellectual elite, a point which leads nicely to the counterargument.

On the opposite end of the spectrum from the "language snobs" are the "language slobs" (Williams). As the linguistic conservatives are trying desperately to prevent any kind of change in the language, these radicals believe that the "rules of language reflect the reality of human speech" and to attempt to control the language is to attempt to control the culture. Rather than make society follow the rails of a preserved language, they believe language should follow the flow of popular culture. Doing otherwise would be detrimental to creative expression. In fact, the present politics of academia have "been on the side of an open-ended diversity" in that grammar is now seen as a "plot to perpetuate the political dominance of white males." The teaching of grammar is suddenly politically incorrect as these radicals view it as preventing students from expressing themselves in their own "idioms and style and punctuation." Of course, strong individual voices would struggle to come out of a shaky verbal foundation in the first place, but "expression without form" is hardly as dire a consequence as "form without [...] energy" (Williams). This is the real issue. The inconsequential changes that are disconcerting some to no end are just that—inconsequential.

"Word Orthodoxy" has no place in our current society (Adams). Such borders sever creative extremities and are not capable of containing something that is so intrinsically tied to our forever-evolving society. Of course proper grammar is an essential tool in the creation of artistic literature. However, this grammatical dogma is more of a limiting tool than a constructive one. If your inner monologue is constantly reciting "I shall not..." and "never, ever...," it's awfully difficult to hear "what if..." or "maybe I could..." My seventh-grade teacher would have found three travesties of grammatical justice in this paper. Rather narrow, isn't it?

Works Cited

Adams, Rob. "Comments on 'Orwellian.'" 28 Jan. 2003. *Provenance: Unknown.* Ed. Matt Pfeffer. 9 Nov. 2003 <http://www. provenanceunknown.com/archive/2003/01-27_orwellian.html>.

"Clues to Concise Writing." *Vocabula Review* 3.2 (Feb. 2001). 9 Nov. 2003 <http://www.vocabula.com/vrFEB01concise.htm>.

Eakin, Emily. "Going at the Changes in, Ya Know, English." *New York Times* 15 Nov. 2003. 15 Nov. 2003 <http://www.nytimes.com>.

Kurland, Dan. "Words: Our Evolving Language." *How the Language Really Works: The Fundamentals of Critical Reading and Effective Writing.* (2000). 9 Nov. 2003 <http:// www.critical-reading.com/words.htm>.

Nunberg, Geoffrey. "The Decline of Grammar." *Atlantic Monthly* Dec. 1983: 31–44.

Orwell, George. "Politics and the English Language." May 1945. George Orwell, 1903–1950: Work: Essays. 6 Nov. 2003 <http://www.k-1.com/Orwell/index.cgi/work/essays/language.html>.

Safire, William. "Quotations by Author." *The Quotation Page.* 9 Nov. 2003 <http://www.quotationspage.com/quotes/William_Safire>.

Society for the Preservation of English Language and Literature. Homepage. 9 Nov. 2003 <http://www.spellorg.com>.

Williams, David R. "Snobs and Slobs." *Vocabula Review* 3.2 (Feb. 2001). 9 Nov. 2003. <http://www.vocabula.com/vrFEB01williams.htm>.

Appendix A

PWR Course Policies

The following are general course policies that apply to all PWR courses. However, because there may be some variation in the way instructors choose to implement them, it is your responsibility to consult your course syllabus and instructor about particular policies for your class.

PWR Course Policies

Enrollment

Capped at just eighteen students, First-Year Writing and Rhetoric is likely to be one of the smallest classes you take at CU. The PWR believes strongly that writing courses should be kept small so that students can work closely with their instructor and also with one another on their writing. PWR instructors are therefore asked not to over-enroll their courses. If you find yourself on a waitlist, you have several options: you can stay on the waitlist in hopes that an enrolled student drops the course during the drop/add period; you can stay on the waitlist in order to be eligible for course reservation the following semester (guidelines for course reservation are online at http://registrar.colorado.edu); or you can look for a section with openings. Staff in the PWR main office can help you decide which is the best option.

Adds/Drops

You must attend your class regularly during the drop/add period. Any student who misses two classes during that period *may* be administratively dropped in order to make space for students on the waiting list. However, this process is not automatic, so if you decide you don't want to take the class, it is your responsibility to drop it in order to avoid receiving an "F" for the course.

Attendance

In a class as small as this one, your absence will be noticed. Other students depend on your feedback in class discussions and workshops. In short, *your presence counts in this course.* While *any* absence may affect your grade, most instructors designate a maximum number of classes you can miss before they officially begin deducting points from your final grade. Thus it is very important that you become familiar with your instructor's particular guidelines and policies for attendance, and that you use your absences wisely, saving some for illness or an emergency late in the semester.

If you must miss a class, you are responsible for finding out what you missed and for keeping up with the assignments. If you know in advance that you will have to miss a class, it's a good idea to let your instructor know *ahead of time* by e-mail or, better yet, by making an appointment with him or her. (E-mailing your instructor after the fact to ask, "What did I miss?" isn't a good option. Your instructor doesn't have the time to summarize an entire class period or workshop in an e-mail!)

If you need to be absent for a religious observance or for military obligations, you must give your instructor two weeks' notice. In the case of a military obligation, you will need a note from an officer verifying the reason for your absence. You will also need to arrange in advance for any work that needs to be completed.

Faculty Mailboxes

All work should be turned in during class time unless you have made other arrangements with your instructor in advance. In the event that you do need to turn in an assignment outside of regular class time, all PWR instructors have a mailbox in the lobby of the building where their office is located (either in the basement of Environmental Design or in Temporary Building 1). Please note, however, that mailboxes are only accessible during regular business hours: Monday–Friday, 8 a.m.–5 p.m.

Lateness

Individual instructors' policies on lateness vary; check your course syllabus to find out what the policy is for your class. Generally, walking in late or leaving early displays disregard for the class. If you know that you will be late for a class or will have to leave early, let your instructor know ahead of time. Also, be aware that many instructors count late arrivals or early departures as absences. The same goes for turning work in late. Instructors are not required to accept late work; at the very least, most require that you make arrangements with them in advance.

Appealing a Grade

If you have questions about the grade you receive on a particular assignment or for the course, the first step is to make an appointment with your instructor so that the two of you can discuss your concerns. If, after speaking with your instructor, you believe that the grade you have received is unfair given the assignment or course objectives, you may follow the PWR's process for appealing a grade:

Step one: You may submit a formal, written appeal to the PWR conflict resolution coordinator. (Please see contact information on page iii at the beginning of this book.) All appeals must be made within 45 days of the academic term in which the course was taken.

Step two: If the conflict resolution coordinator deems a review appropriate, he or she will evaluate all relevant course information. It is your responsibility to provide the coordinator with copies of relevant documents (e.g., course policies, syllabus, assignments, clean copies of papers). The coordinator will then have two other PWR instructors independently read and evaluate the paper(s) in question.

The conflict resolution coordinator will speak with you and your instructor about the outcome of the review. The instructor will take the review under advisement in deciding whether or not to change the grade.

Step three: If you are still not satisfied with the outcome of the appeals process, you may then take the matter to the director of the Program for Writing and Rhetoric, who, after reviewing the case, will make his or her recommendation to the instructor. Final authority for any grade rests with the instructor.

English as a Second Language
The PWR dedicates certain sections of its first-year courses for students whose native language is not English; these sections are distinguished by an 800 section number. These sections have the same goals as the standard sections but may address issues of particular concern to non-native writers of English. If you are a nonnative writer of English, you may prefer to take these classes for a variety of reasons: You may wish to reinforce your understanding of American academic writing; you may want an opportunity to write and read about language differences; or you may feel the need for more formal attention to English grammar and style. If you're unsure whether an 800 section is suitable for you, come by the PWR main office on the lower level of Environmental Design in room 1B60, or call the PWR office at 303-492-8188.

Special Accommodations
If you qualify for accommodations because of a disability, please submit to your instructor a letter from Disability Services in a timely manner so that your needs may be addressed. Disability Services determines accommodations based on documented disabilities (303-492-8671, Willard 322, www.colorado.edu/disabilityservices).

Plagiarism
Plagiarism is the act of passing off another's work as your own. Stealing, buying, or otherwise using someone else's work, in whole or in part, constitutes plagiarism and is against university policy. Such behavior is taken seriously by the Honors Council, to which many such incidents are referred. Consult www.colorado.edu/academics/honorcode/ to learn more about the CU Honor Code.

Plagiarism does not always take such blatant forms, however. Of equal concern, especially in a course like this one where you will be *encouraged* to draw on others' ideas in your own writing, are the more subtle forms of plagiarism. For example, you probably know that all words taken directly from a source need to be quoted and cited, and that there are specific conventions for doing this properly. However, you may not know that merely changing a few words in a passage—say, by using the thesaurus function on your word-processing program—does not protect you from the charge of plagiarism. Passages that are similar to their sources in syntax, organization, or wording but are not cited are considered to be plagiarized. In fact, even if you cite the source but do not make it clear to your readers that the phrasing of a passage is not your own, the source is still considered to be plagiarized.

Any time you use another's work—ideas, theories, statistics, graphs, photos, or facts that are not common knowledge—you must acknowledge the author.

Depending on the severity of the offense and on the instructor's particular policy, the consequences for plagiarism vary, from having to rewrite a section of a paper to receiving a failing grade. Therefore, in addition to making sure you understand what constitutes an offense, it is important that you become familiar with your instructor's policy.

In the PWR, we see plagiarism as more than merely a matter of policy or legality. It is also an issue of respect and regard for other readers and writers. Some students are reluctant to cite their sources because they mistakenly believe that in college all their ideas must be original. But the university is a community of thinkers; as such, the writing we produce may be thought of as a conversation with other thinkers. As in any conversation, your "listeners" expect you to build on what has already been said.

We all build on each other's ideas, making our own small contribution to the discussion. At the same time, we all like to see our ideas acknowledged. Acknowledging other people's work can only enhance your reputation as a credible, thoughtful, honest writer. Although the ideas in your paper may come from others, the way you put them together and make sense of them will be uniquely your own.

Appendix B

Campus Resources for Writers

The PWR and University Libraries are committed to providing support for writers at all levels, through a range of resources. We encourage you to take advantage of these resources—not just while you are enrolled in a writing course, but throughout your college career.

PWR Resources

PWR Conflict Resolution

We provide a confidential conflict resolution service for students of the Program for Writing and Rhetoric. Students may consult with the conflict resolution coordinator about perceived problems in their PWR courses without their instructor's knowledge. The PWR conflict resolution coordinator will help settle disputes and personality conflicts between students and instructors. The coordinator will also handle student challenges to a grade, plagiarism concerns, and similar problems that may arise in PWR classes. To contact the PWR conflict resolution coordinator, see the information on page iii at the beginning of this book.

Writing Center

We are a faculty of professional writing consultants available to help you through the writing process. Better yet, our help is free to CU students! Writing consultants have experience teaching writing at the collegiate level and are trained to help individual writers improve their skills. We encourage you to take advantage of this great benefit, not only while you are enrolled in the first-year writing course, but throughout your college career.

Our consultants are on hand to help you at any stage of the writing process, from brainstorming and organizing your ideas to finally understanding the mysteries of grammar and style. Please do keep in mind that the Writing Center is *not* an editing service; our goal is to teach you to become more skillful and aware as a writer by using your own papers as tutorials.

We ask that you bring your draft, outline or notes, and the assignment description with you and that you keep papers to a 10-page maximum per visit. Writing Center consultations last 50 minutes and should be booked in advance.

To book an appointment, please visit our website (www.colorado.edu/pwr/writingcenter.html). You'll need to register for a free account to access our appointment calendar. Once registered, you'll have the ability to book up to two appointments per week.

One caution, though: Don't wait until the last minute to seek help; we have a limited number of consultants, and the time slots often fill quickly, especially at midterms and the end of the semester. We advise booking at least a few days in advance.

We are located in Norlin Library room E-156 right next the revolving doors at the east entrance. Please visit our website for more information about our hours and contact information: www.colorado.edu/pwr/writingcenter.html

PWR Website Links to Online Resources
In addition to resources that your instructor and the CU's library staff provide, you can find a list of online writing and research resources on the PWR website at: http://www.colorado.edu/pwr/resources.html. Click on "Writing and Research Links."

Library Resources

Library PWR Website
The website for the information literacy component of First-Year Writing and Rhetoric is available at http://ucblibraries.colorado.edu/pwr/. As this is a long URL and can be difficult to remember, here is another way to access the website:

1. Go to the Library home page at http://ucblibraries.colorado.edu.
2. On the far right side, there is an A–Z listing titled "About the Libraries."
3. Select the letter "P." From this list, select "PWR (Program for Writing and Rhetoric)."

This page includes links to all of the other online resources you'll need for First-Year Writing and Rhetoric, including the reading themes and online tutorials and quizzes (RIOT). If at any point you have a question about how to access these resources, please e-mail pwrhelp@colorado.edu.

Reading Themes and Research Tutorials (RIOT)
The PWR Research Tutorials (RIOT) are located at http://ucblibraries.colorado.edu/pwr/tutorial/home.htm. In addition to the tutorials, the library also provides a list of Reading Themes for the PWR: a list of links to articles, websites, and other resources grouped together by topic. Depending on your instructor, you may or may not be assigned readings from this list, but you may want to check them out anyway as a possible resource for your own research. They can be found at http://ucblibraries.colorado.edu/pwr/themes/themes.htm. Both of these resources can also be accessed through the links on the library's PWR page (see address above).

Remote Access

You will have no difficulty accessing the library resources such as the reading themes and tutorials from a campus computer. However, if you are using an off-campus computer (your home computer, for example), the system will not recognize that you are a CU student and you will be denied access. To correct this problem, you must establish remote access. To find out how, go to http://ucblibraries.colorado.edu/research/remote.htm and follow the directions. If at any time you have questions about remote access, please call the ITS Help Line at (303) 735-HELP. A final note, AOL does not work with the library sources; please use Internet Explorer, Netscape, or a similar browser.

Drop-in Research Center

The Drop-in Research Center, located in the Norlin Library, provides assistance with accessing reading themes, completing the library tutorials, and any other research needs you may have. The staff of the Research Center will help you learn to use available library resources by providing one-on-one help. Please check the webpage http://ucblibraries.colorado.edu/pwr/ for information on the hours and location of the Research Center.

Reference Desk

If you cannot make it to the Drop-in Research Center, stop by the Norlin Library Reference Desk, which is staffed by librarians who provide general and specialized research help. Please come to the desk whenever you need assistance with your research. The Reference Desk is located on the first floor in the northeast corner. It is open Monday–Friday 9 a.m.–9 p.m. and Saturday–Sunday 1–5 p.m.

PWR Writing Contest

The PWR holds a contest each year for the best writing in its core classes. If you have a piece you would like to submit, see your teacher for the submission guidelines and deadline. You may obtain a contest entry form by going to the PWR homepage (www.colorado.edu/pwr/) and clicking on "Resources." In addition to receiving cash prizes, winning entries will be published in the PWR's online journal, *Occasions*, and they may also be selected to appear in the next edition of *Knowing Words*. Several of the essays included in Chapter 5—including "Makeover Feminism," "Cultural Chameleon," and "Learning to Read"—were selected from among past years' submissions. Good Luck!

PWR Cover Art Contest

In addition to the writing contest, PWR holds an annual student cover art contest. The contest is open to all CU undergraduate students—you do not need to be enrolled in a writing course to enter. The contest winner receives a cash prize, and the winning art piece becomes the cover for the next edition of *Knowing Words*. You may obtain a contest entry form by going to the PWR homepage (www.colorado.edu/pwr/) and clicking on "Resources." Submission guidelines and deadlines are listed on the form. Good Luck!